SUCCESSFUL
SALTWATER
AQUARIUMS

A BEGINNER'S GUIDE

BY

JOHN H. TULLOCK

A CORALIFE ® PUBLICATION

Energy Savers Unlimited, Inc., Harbor City, CA

Cover photo courtesy of Pierre Catellier

ISBN 0-9640147-0-X
Printed in the United States of America

DEDICATION

For Dad, who first showed me the wonders a
single drop of water can contain.

Contents

FOREWORD

The evolution of the aquarium hobby has taken us from the sterile, hospital-like, fish tank to the reef aquarium. Reef aquarium keeping has become one of the fastest growing areas of the hobby. Concurrent with this evolution has been the development of an entire technology aimed at the maintenance of reef creatures. Many of these technological advances have benefited not only the reef keeping segment of the hobby, but have been adapted for use in other types of aquaria. Aquariums whose primary aim is to maintain a collection of fishes are now being fitted with trickle filters, protein skimmers, redox controllers and even "live rock." As a result, many fishes once thought difficult or impossible to maintain are thriving for years. Advances in our knowledge of nutritional requirements for various fishes and invertebrates have led to the development of appropriate foods. The production of synthetic aquarium salt has been refined. These advances have made captive propagation of many species possible. In the not too distant future, most aquarium species will be hatchery produced. Despite the advances achieved, this "technological" stage in the evolution of the marine hobby has placed too little emphasis on understanding the biology of the animals and how they interact with their aquatic environment.

This book addresses the maintenance of healthy marine aquariums. Rather than merely describing the most recent advances of aquarium technology, Tullock concentrates primarily on the requirements of the animals. He has been one of the leading advocates of a "natural" approach to marine reef keeping in particular, and aquarium keeping in general. His refreshing approach in *Successful Saltwater Aquariums* is eloquently yet simply presented. Beginning hobbyists and "old salts" alike will benefit from its reading. Several chapters are aimed primarily at the beginner, including a section on basic equipment and one on routine maintenance. The chapter on water chemistry is clear and concise, answering questions in an easy to understand fashion. Nearly half of the book consists of descriptions of common fish and invertebrate families available to hobbyists. A general discussion of invertebrate care introduces the invertebrate section. The text includes a description of the compatibility of invertebrates with other aquarium inhabitants, and their suitability in various types of aquarium setups.

Because John Tullock is both a retail merchant and widely-recognized author, he frequently receives questions from hobbyists on various aspects of marine aquarium keeping. Chapter 8 of this book is dedicated to the most frequently asked questions. This is another section that hobbyists new to marine aquariums will find very informative.

There is no single tool that is better than knowledge to insure success in any endeavor. This is especially true of marine aquarium keeping. *Successful Salt-*

water Aquariums is a good tool. You will refer to it time and time again!

> J. R. Shute
> Knoxville, Tennessee
> December 20, 1993

(J.R. Shute is the Vice-President of Aquatic Specialists, and coauthors "The Marine Team" with John Tullock each month in Tropical Fish Hobbyist.*)*

PREFACE

When Lee Eng brought chunks of rock with attached encrusting organisms from the ocean near his home in Jakarta, Indonesia and placed them in his aquarium, he was not aware that he would be remembered as the first person to create a living reef aquarium. That was in the 1960's, when marine aquariums were a rarity in the homes of American hobbyists. Today, of course, marine aquarium keeping is a popular hobby for thousands of people, although the keeping of reef invertebrates is still restricted to relatively few enthusiasts. With the increase in interest in aquariums displaying fishes and, especially, invertebrates, from coral reef habitats, there has been a parallel proliferation of products for filtering, lighting, and maintaining them. Many of these products have indeed made the establishment and maintenance of marine aquariums easier. Some, perhaps, have actually made matters more difficult.

This book is very different from my first effort, *The Reef Tank Owner's Manual*. The difference lies primarily in a growing awareness on my part that the enjoyment of coral reef invertebrates in the home aquarium had to be simpler and less costly than it was at the time *RTOM* made its debut (April, 1991). I began to learn all I could about so-called "Berlin-method" aquariums. Peter Wilkens, Julian Sprung, Charles Delbeek, and others had written about this approach, and I decided to try it myself. The results I achieved were so satisfactory that I abandoned the old methods of "filtration" that I had been employing, indeed that I had written about in *RTOM*, and set about perfecting a "natural" reef tank methodology. I have learned a great deal from other aquarists along the way. By and large, however, the experiences and examples I will describe in the pages that follow are my own, or were developed by aquarists at my company, Aquatic Specialists. To each of those dedicated folks, I am grateful. Having grown up on a farm, I can tell you that any enterprise involving living animals is a challenge. With the skills and attention of the rest of the team, we meet that challenge every day. Thanks, you guys.

My goal in sharing this information with hobbyists is to encourage them to apply these techniques to your own aquarium. I hope that the result will be as much pleasure as I have experienced. I also hope that your aquarium experience will sharpen your interest in learning about all of the creatures of the sea, including those that we could never have in our homes. As your knowledge deepens, I am sure that you will share my view that these creatures, along with all the others with whom we share this planet, need our respect and our protection.

In offering you the techniques for creating a "natural" aquarium, I have not neglected the needs of the aquarium hobbyist who prefers to keep what I now call an "artificial" system. This type of marine aquarium is more traditional, featuring mostly coral reef fishes and decorations other than live rock and sessile invertebrates. I have learned that there are a great many hobbyists across America that are still having problems keeping marine fishes alive and thriving in systems such as these. This is unfortunate, and, many times, represents a needless waste of marine life. I have tried to present a basic approach to this type of marine aquarium that emphasizes an understanding of the natural adaptations of different fish species.

I would like to acknowledge the help and advice of a great many people who have, in one way or another, had a role in the development of the ideas presented in this book. Some names, Julian Sprung and Martin Moe, for example, would be instantly recognized by most marine enthusiasts. Others, like Dr. David Etnier and the late Dr. Orvin Mundt, would be less familiar. And many of my ideas have been developed as a result of telephone conversations with hobbyists whose names I never knew. To all of these people, my heartfelt thanks. Finally, credit is due to Omer Dersom, President of Energy Savers Unlimited, Inc., for recognizing the need for a book such as this. Thanks, Omer, for your encouragement and support.

John H. Tullock
Knoxville, Tennessee
December 10, 1993

Chapter One
INTRODUCTION

You've been bitten by the saltwater bug, haven't you? Every time you visit your dealer, you are captivated by the absolutely gorgeous saltwater fish and invertebrates on display. You've kept freshwater fish successfully for several years, and, up until now, you've resisted the temptation to set up a saltwater tank.

Other hobbyists have related horror stories, and these have served to dampen your enthusiasm for the denizens of coral reefs. "They only live a few weeks," some say. "You've got to fuss with the tank every minute," others whine. "One little mistake, and everything in the tank is dead," a fellow hobbyist warns, " I gave up and went back to breeding *Synodontis* catfishes. I wanted something easier." You hear these conversations repeated in your head as you gaze into the dealer's tank. An exquisitely beautiful mandarin fish floats just above the bottom, propelled by the constant movement of its translucent blue fins. From underneath a rock nearby, a gaudy little neon goby peeks out. Pink anemones sway in the water currents. You can't resist any longer...you're going to set up a marine tank.

I will not add my voice to those who would discourage you. On the contrary, marine aquariums have given me tremendous pleasure for the past twenty years or so. However, I would discourage you from launching into the marine hobby without first giving some serious thought to the undertaking. A marine aquarium will require more of your time than a freshwater tank, but your time will be well-rewarded. Provided, that is, that you make an effort initially to learn about marine aquariums, and to plan your marine tank carefully.

For starters, read a book. This brief guide can help steer you in the right direction, but there is no substitute for knowledge when it comes to marine aquarium keeping, and books are your best source of all the basic information in one convenient place. Titles you might consider are:

Mills, Dick (1987) *The Tetra Encyclopedia of the Marine Aquarium*, Salamander Books, Ltd., Morris Plains, NJ. 208 pp. Illus.

Moe, Martin A., Jr. (1982) *The Marine Aquarium Handbook, Beginner to Breeder*. Green Turtle Publications, Plantation, FL. 170 pp. Illus.

If you think you might like to have a tank primarily for invertebrates, do not think that this can only be done with complex and expensive filtration and lighting systems. True, corals and some of the other choices for "reef tanks" are not for the beginner, but there are a host of invertebrate species that can be included in a simple, small and entertaining set-up. For ideas about setting up an invertebrate aquarium, consult any of the following:

Moe, Martin A., Jr. (1989) *The Marine Aquarium Reference, Systems and Invertebrates.* Green Turtle Publications, Plantation, FL. 510 pp. Illus.

Prasek, Edward (1993) *The Beginner's Guide to Micro and Minireef Systems.* Aardvark Press, Mesilla Park, NM. 70 pp.

Thiel, Albert (1989) *Small Reef Aquarium Basics.* Aardvark Press, Bridgeport, CT. 170 pp. Illus.

Tullock, John H. (1992) *The Reef Tank Owner's Manual.* Second Edition, Revised. Aardvark Press, Mesilla Park, NM. 272 pp. Illus.

As you read one (or preferably, all) of these books, make notes. Create a list of fish and/or invertebrate species that you think you might like to keep. Write down questions that arise, points about which you feel you need more information or a better explanation. Also, decide how much money, space, and time you can devote to your marine aquarium. In this way, you will develop a plan that will guide you when you begin purchasing equipment, and later, specimens. If you have a well thought out plan in hand before you actually begin, you will spare yourself some frustration, not to mention expense, when you actually install and stock your new marine tank.

In developing your plan, keep the following five points in mind:

1. Keep it simple.

As a novice, you should be paying more attention to maintaining good water quality, providing proper nutrition for your specimens, and carrying out routine maintenance, and less attention to installing the latest piece of high-tech equipment. Make no mistake, none of the fancy equipment currently available will substitute for proper husbandry on the part of the aquarist. Start with a basic system and learn to maintain it properly. Then you will be better able to decide wisely if additional equipment will really help you to get more enjoyment out of your tank. In later chapters, we will explore the proper utilization of specialized equipment.

2. Keep it roomy.

Marine fishes require ample space. Even the largest aquarium is tiny in comparison to the vastness of the ocean around a coral reef. The size tank you choose will, most likely, be determined by the space and budget you have available. Therefore, if you only have room for a ten gallon tank, don't set your heart on a fish that requires a fifty gallon tank. Plan to keep species that are in proportion to the size of the captive ocean you are contemplating.

3. Keep it stable.

Apart from the abyssal depths of the ocean, the coral reef environment (from which come virtually all of the fish and invertebrate species offered for sale in the aquarium trade) is among the most stable on earth. Reef fishes and invertebrates have therefore not evolved adaptive strategies to cope with rapid fluctuations in environmental conditions. This is in marked contrast to freshwater fishes, which generally come from rivers, streams and lakes that may experience quite drastic changes throughout the course of a normal year. Maintaining stability in a marine tank means basically that you must have reliable equipment, and you must perform required maintenance consistently.

4. Keep it clean.

Feed sparingly, and remove dead organic matter promptly. Siphon out detritus on a regular basis. This chore is usually done in conjunction with removing water for a routine water change. Above all, do not allow pollutants to accumulate in the tank. Pollutants can be generated within the tank (compounds such as ammonia,nitrite and nitrate, about which we will have much to say in a future chapter), as well as from outside the tank (household chemicals, improperly used medications and additives, and sometimes pollutants in tap water). One of the major physiological differences between marine fish and their freshwater counterparts is their relationship to the watery medium in which they live. In freshwater fishes, the body fluids are "saltier" than the water surrounding them. Freshwater fish constantly absorb water by osmosis, and are thus always in physiological danger of fluid overload. To compensate for this, freshwater fishes rarely drink water, and their kidneys excrete copious quantities of very dilute urine to rid their bodies of the excess water. Marine fishes, on the other hand, have body fluids that are less "salty" than the seawater surrounding them. Thus, they lose water to their surroundings, and, ironically, are in constant danger of dehydration. To compensate, marine fishes drink large amounts of seawater, and excrete relatively small amounts of concentrated urine. In either marine or freshwater fishes, only water itself enters or leaves the tissues via osmosis. Substances in the water generally must enter the body via ingestion. Since they ingest water continually, marine fishes are therefore much more susceptible to poisoning from waterborne pollutants than freshwater fishes are. For example, copper is often used in freshwater tanks to control algae growth, at a concentration of about 1 part per million, and freshwater fishes are not affected by its presence. However, copper is toxic to most marine fishes at a concentration roughly three or four times lower than this.

5. Keep it natural.

Try to duplicate, as closely as possible, the conditions under which your marine specimens would live in nature. This means, basically, that you should endeavor to thoroughly investigate the requirements of any species in which you are interested before you purchase a specimen.

Your new marine aquarium has the potential to afford you years of enjoyment and satisfaction. By following the five simple rules I have outlined above, you can begin having fun, and not frustration, from the outset. In order to obtain both equipment and specimens for your new marine tank, you will need to do some shopping. Visit every dealer in your area, but do not shop simply to locate the cheapest price, especially for fish. One dealer may have a particular piece of equipment on sale at a bargain price, and you have little to lose in taking advantage of such a special "deal". However, much of your long term success with marine aquarium keeping will depend upon the quality of both information and livestock that your dealer provides, and this can vary quite widely, indeed.

Here are some guidelines to help you in selecting a quality dealer for marine fish and invertebrates:

• Look for a dealer that has a large number of tanks devoted to saltwater specimens, in relation to

the overall stock of fishes.

In some cities, there are dealers that sell only marines, but this is hardly the rule. A large selection of saltwater specimens usually indicates that the dealer is doing a brisk saltwater business, which implies that many other customers have been satisfied with the quality of the service and specimens provided.

• **Examine closely the condition of the specimens in the dealer's tanks.**

Are they active, alert, undamaged, free from signs of disease? Apply the same criteria to marine fish that you would apply when seeking healthy freshwater specimens.

• **Note especially whether the dealer quarantines marine specimens for a period of time before offering them for sale, or if specimens that arrived last night are hustled out the door this morning.**

Remember that the bulk of marine specimens are caught in the wild. Capture and shipment, often for thousands of miles, is very stressful for fishes, and they need a period of rest and recovery before being netted again, dumped in a bag and sent home with a novice aquarist. Devoting tank space to quarantine fishes that the dealer has already paid for costs him or her considerable money. You can expect to pay more for the same specimen in such a store, but, I promise, it will be worth it in the long run.

• Visit the store when business is slow, and ask questions.

Tell the clerk that you are considering a saltwater tank for the first time, and that you want to learn about the hobby before you begin. If all you receive in return is a sales pitch for a giant tank with a complex, expensive filtration system, leave at the first opportunity, and find another store that demonstrates a sincere interest in your success with the marine hobby. Don't expect any dealer, however, to spend a lot of time with you when the store is packed with customers. Come back another day.

• When you visit a store for the first time, come prepared with a couple of questions for which, from your reading, you already know the correct answer.

You can quickly determine if this store has knowledgeable personnel and dispenses good advice. There are, of course, legitimate differences of opinion among experienced marine aquarists about certain aspects of aquarium keeping. Nevertheless, there is, at least among most experts on the subject, practically universal agreement on a number of key points. If you read several books and magazine articles devoted to marine aquarium keeping, you will easily discover these.

If the store you visit seems consistently to provide information that is at variance with accepted practices and common sense, find another store.

You will need to invest some time in locating a good dealer for marine specimens. Once you have made your choice, reward that store's efforts with your patronage. The business of selling marine fishes is fraught with risk and difficulty, and may not be particularly profitable, in comparison to, for example, a dress shop. Any dealer who makes the effort to provide you with good quality specimens, courteous service, and sound advice deserves to remain in business. And he or she can only do so if you shop there. In the next chapter, I will discuss the basic equipment needed to maintain marine organisms successfully in the aquarium. You can begin your marine aquarium right now. Read, plan, shop, ask questions, and make notes. Patience at this stage will be amply rewarded.

TULLOCK'S FIVE RULES FOR A SUCCESSFUL MARINE AQUARIUM

1. **KEEP IT SIMPLE.**

2. **KEEP IT ROOMY.**

3. **KEEP IT STABLE.**

4. **KEEP IT CLEAN.**

5. **KEEP IT NATURAL.**

Chapter Two
BASIC EQUIPMENT

I shall take the liberty to assume that you have some knowledge of aquariums, although you may never have kept one before. To successfully maintain marine organisms in the home for any reasonable length of time, you will of course need an aquarium of some kind. This can be a tank of any size, but the bigger the better. Since the aquarium will weigh about ten pounds per gallon when filled, it will need a sturdy support near both electricity and a sink. The tank should be made entirely of glass or acrylic. You will also need a cover for the tank.

Temperature Control

Temperature control is vital to the success of a tropical marine aquarium. Purchase a heater of sufficient wattage to keep the aquarium at a constant 75° F. About three watts per gallon is usually satisfactory. The higher the wattage, for a given number of gallons being heated, the faster the temperature of the water will rise when the heater is on. Sudden temperature shifts are to be avoided; therefore, do not select a heater that is of a higher wattage than that recommended. You may require a chiller if the tank does not remain below 80°. A chiller can represent a significant investment, but, if necessary to keep the tank in the proper temperature range, it is an indispensible component of the aquarium system.

Accessories

You will need an assortment of accessories for aquarium maintenance chores. Some of these items, surprisingly, are seldom sold at aquarium shops, and you will need to visit the local hardware or discount store. Items such as buckets that will be in contact with aquarium water should be clearly labeled as such and used only for this purpose, to avoid inadvertently contaminating the aquarium. I suggest treating aquarium equipment as you would treat food handling equipment in your kitchen. By the same token, if you would deem a particular container suitable for food storage, it should also be acceptable for storing aquarium water, dry salt mix, etc. Here is a suggested list of maintenance equipment:

• **Five gallon buckets, with lids, for storing and handling seawater. (You will need at least two, and perhaps several, depending upon the size tank you have.)**

• A plastic container of 30 - 50 gallons, for mixing and storing seawater. (Plastic garbage cans work well; choose one with a snug-fitting lid.)

• About 6 feet of clear vinyl hose, for use as a siphon. (Aquarium shops carry siphons fitted with a long funnel-like accessory that is very useful for removing debris from the tank.)

• Clear, rectangular plastic containers of various sizes for capturing and moving aquarium specimens. (Aquarium shops often use "catch cups" made just for this purpose. Do not use nets for moving marine fish and invertebrates, as you risk damaging the specimen. Along the same lines, never remove specimens from the water; this can also damage them significantly.)

You will no doubt find use for various other tools to make aquarium maintenance easier. I will offer suggestions for handy tools throughout the text whenever a particular procedure is first mentioned.

In addition to the tank itself and its temperature control system, you will also need both a filtration system and a lighting system. You should give considerable thought to the selection of these components, as filtration and proper lighting are essential to the survival of tropical marine fish and invertebrates. There is a tendency to regard marine fish as "tougher", somehow, than invertebrates. On the contrary, my experience indicates that fish can be more demanding. In any case, we should not think of these two groups as having separate requirements. Water conditions, temperature and lighting cycles should be the same for both. Perhaps the only way in which certain invertebrates are exceptional is their requirement for high light intensity (more about this later). Fish, while they do not *require* high intensity lighting, nevertheless benefit from it.

The Logic of Aquarium Filtration

When you think about filtration equipment for a new marine aquarium, think about *nutrients*. That's right, nutrients. There are not very many nutrients in the waters around coral reefs. The novice saltwater enthusiast should never forget that all of the life forms that will inhabit the marine aquarium will come from the waters around coral reefs. Most of what you will be doing when you care for your marine aquarium will be involved with removing nutrients from the water in the tank. Therefore, think about nutrients, for a moment.

*****

Nutrients are, of course, essential for the survival of most living organisms. However, one of the special features of the coral reef environment is the paucity of nutrients in the water. Reef organisms have developed marvelously efficient ways to capture, and in many cases to recycle, most of the available nutrients, with the result that the bulk of the *nitrogen*, *phosphorus*, and *organic carbon* present in the reef habitat is found in the *biomass*, not dissolved in the water. In the aquarium, which is a closed system and an ecologically incomplete environment even under the best of circumstances, excess nutrients begin to accumulate from the moment living organisms are added. This accumulation results in a decline in the water quality of the system. If nothing is done to reverse this process, water conditions will soon deteriorate to a point outside the range of tolerance of the lifeforms, and they, in turn, will fare poorly. Filtration is therefore necessary to prevent, or at least retard, this gradual worsening of the water conditions. Filtration, properly chosen and combined with water changes and the judicious application of certain tank additives, enables the aquarist to maintain aquarium water in good condition almost indefinitely.

The Logic of Aquarium Lighting

Sunlight plays an important role in the nutrient recycling process that naturally occurs on coral reefs, and this fact has important implications in the selection of aquarium lighting. If any of the aquarium inhabitants are of the sort that carry out photosynthesis, and this group includes many of the most desirable invertebrates, lighting must be of high intensity and of a suitable spectrum. If these organisms will not be included in your aquarium, the simple fluorescent lighting fixtures that are sold in aquarium shops are quite satisfactory.

I will have more to say about special aquarium lighting in a moment. If your tank will be one with no special lighting needs, consider the selection of the *lamp* as well as the fixture, for a moment. Fluorescent lamps (the replaceable white tube that fits into the light fixture) can vary in two ways, by *wattage* and by *type* . You should understand both of these terms. A fluorescent fixture is designed to accommodate lamps of a certain wattage. Lamps of differing wattages are usually of different lengths (see table at the end of this chapter), and only the correct wattage will fit the fixture. For a given wattage, however, there may be many types of lamps. Fluorescent lamp types are identified with a variety of brand names, and with a coded designation printed on one end of the lamp. Different types vary in their brightness (intensity) and in the spectral quality ("color") of the light they produce. Since these characteristics are not important for a simple set-up that will have no photosynthetic organisms present, I suggest you view an aquarium illuminated by various lamp types, and choose the one you think looks best.

Selecting Filtration and Lighting Equipment

Choosing suitable filtration and lighting is only one aspect of setting up a successful saltwater aquarium, but it is a very important aspect, for two reasons. First, a significant portion of the total cost of the aquarium will be spent for the filtration and lighting systems. Second, there is a trade-off between the initial investment in equipment, and the amount of effort you will later expend in keeping the tank in shape. Such effort may not only involve maintenance chores, but, alas, may also be associated with medicating sick fish, replacing filter media and light bulbs, coping with prolific algae growth, and repairing worn or faulty equipment. The time to be choosy and critical is now, when you are first setting up the tank, not six months from now when that bargain-priced pump fails while you are away for the weekend.

There is such a bewildering array of options available for filtering a marine tank. Which one is "best"? The correct answer, of course, is that no one filtration system is suitable for all applications, and that the choice for your particular aquarium should be determined by what you intend to keep in the tank. There are probably as many filtration theories as there are aquarists, but for simplicity's sake, I will discuss only three approaches to marine tank filtration. These I shall call "high-tech",

"natural", and "traditional" set-ups. Thoroughly dedicated marine hobbyists can actually forgo filtration altogether, by the way, provided they are willing to carry
out frequent, large water changes. All any filtration
system can do, really, is extend the useful life of the
water in the tank. And no filtration system, no matter
how sophisticated, can eliminate the need for partial
water changes. All filtration methods are applied with
the intent of preventing changes in the chemistry of the
aquarium water that would render it unsuitable, i.e.,
stress-producing, for the inhabitants of the tank.

"High-tech" filtration systems seek to *automate*,
insofar as possible, maintenance of appropriate water
quality. The goal is stability of the water chemistry,
with minimal labor for the aquarist. The redox controller would receive my vote for most likely centerpiece
of such a system, although only a couple of years ago,
any tank fitted with a wet/dry filter was "high-tech". If
the idea of an automatic garage door opener, an answering machine that calls your pager to let you know you
have a message waiting, or a fax machine that can take
dictation appeals to your tastes, you may be a candidate
for a high-tech aquarium system. To do it right, you
will need a roomy budget, as you might suspect if you've
ever priced one of those answering machines.

"Natural" filtration systems rely primarily on the
good judgement of the aquarist, a protein skimmer, and
ample quantities of live rock. This is my personal
choice, and one I can in good conscience recommend
to the novice. Developing good judgement about ma-

rine aquarium husbandry requires some hands-on experience, but this disadvantage is outweighed by the
fact that the "natural" method is an ideal approach to a
small, low-budget marine system. For the beginner with
a roomy budget, some equipment that will provide a
margin for errors in judgement might be included in the
system, but I do not believe this is necessary for the
aspiring hobbyist who is willing to invest a little time
to learn the techniques of managing such a system.

"Traditional" systems are, in my view, defined by
the use of the undergravel filter. This somewhat-less-
than-satisfactory device has the decided advantages of
being both cheap, and almost foolproof. Its primary
disadvantage is that proper cleaning is difficult to accomplish. Lately, wet/dry filtration systems have received much attention, largely with regard to their
application in maintaining so-called "reef" tanks. Any
marine aquarium, whether "reef" or "fish-only" will
fare better and be easier to maintain if a wet/dry filter
is installed. Since traditionalists will be horrified at
this allegation, and the novice aquarist may be horrified at the cost of a wet/dry filter, let me explain why I
believe there is a decided advantage to this method of
filtration over the more commonplace, and certainly
cheaper, undergravel filter.

We require the filter, at minimum, to process toxic
ammonia into less toxic nitrate via the process known
as *biological filtration*.   If you do not clearly understand what is meant by "biological filtration" as it
applies to aquarium maintenance, stop right here

and read up on the subject. Complete descriptions of this process, which is mediated by bacteria, are found in many books on aquariums, whether freshwater or saltwater. Excellent articles that deal with biological filtration in detail regularly appear in hobbyist magazines, also. I will therefore keep the present discussion quite brief. (See also Chapter Four.)

In a nutshell, your saltwater aquarium filtration system must be able to detoxify the *ammonia* (a form of nitrogen, a nutrient) that will be produced by the inhabitants of the tank, or they will die rather promptly. Both undergravel filters and wet/dry filters easily accomplish biological filtration. Wet/dry filters excel, however, in two ways. They trap detritus in such a manner that it can be removed with much less effort than is required for an undergravel filter, and they are far easier to maintain without disrupting the tank.

A wet/dry filter is essentially a watertight box (*sump*) with a smaller box (*biological chamber*) sitting on top. Water flows from the aquarium by gravity, trickles through the biological chamber, collects in the sump, and is pumped back into the aquarium. The biolgical chamber is filled with pieces of plastic that become colonized by the *beneficial bacteria* that detoxify ammonia. The sump often houses additional filter media, or other equipment, and thus serves as a convenient place to hide this extra hardware underneath the tank, out of sight. The trickling of water through the biological chamber permits maximum contact with the air, allowing essential oxygen to be dissolved in the water, and harmful carbon dioxide to escape. Detritus, which consists mostly of dead bacteria, is trapped in a simple sheet of polyester fiber pad placed at the top of the biological chamber where water from the tank must flow through it. Good filters have a nifty drawer in this position, in order to facilitate periodic cleaning of this pad. Additional detritus accumulates in the sump, beneath the biological chamber, from which it may be siphoned out with minimal disturbance to the tank itself. Maintenance chores are therefore more easily accomplished, and consequently, more regularly performed.

With an undergravel filter, by contrast, all of this stuff, filter media, water pump, detritus, wires, hoses, etc., is in the tank. This not only spoils the appearance, but makes proper cleaning almost impossible without severe imposition upon the peace of mind of the tank's inhabitants.

I have mentioned detritus several times. Why is detritus such a problem? It acts as a "storage depot" for nutrients, and, as I mentioned above, most of what you want a filter to do is eliminate excess nutrients from the aquarium. Phosphorus compounds, of which detritus is a rich storehouse, if allowed to accumulate, will promote thick, obscuring growths of algae. Organic carbon compounds, dissolved in the water, but also found abundantly in detritus, will provide food for undesirable, and possibly disease-producing, bacteria. The water in the tank will be analogous in purity to the air over the Los Angeles freeway, and your aquarium's inhabitants will not thrive.

If you cannot justify the purchase of a wet/dry filter, and must settle for an undergravel system, plan to spend more time maintaining the tank, and resist the temptation to stock a large number of fishes.

Lighting plays a key role in the marine aquarium, but, as I mentioned previously, is only a critical consideration if you plan to keep photosynthetic organisms, including macroalgae ("seaweeds") or certain invertebrates such as sea anemones. An aquarium that will *not* be home to such organisms should nevertheless be brightly illuminated, however. Reef fishes are accustomed to high light levels in their natural habitat, and bright light will promote the growth of beneficial green algae. As you will come to understand, algae can be both a bane and a blessing in a marine aquarium. When selecting a lamp for the simple fluorescent light fixture described above, choose a lamp that has a high *lumen output*. Lumen output is a measure of the lamp's brightness. Sometimes it is hard to select the brightest lamp just by looking at it. Lumen output data is often available, however, from specifications supplied by the lamp's manufacturer. For a simple lighting system, strive for a pleasing appearance with lighting that is as bright as possible, given the limitations of the fixture (only one or two lamps of standard wattage).

If you plan on keeping anemones, or any other organisms which require bright light, you should consider fixtures that permit you to place several fluorescent lamps over the tank, or perhaps a *metal halide* lighting system.

TABLE 2-1
FLUORESCENT LAMP SIZES
AND WATTAGES

LENGTH IN INCHES	WATTAGE
18	15
24	20
36	30
48	40
72	56
96	75

DECIPHERING LAMP CODES

Here's what a typical lamp code looks like:

F40T12/50U

Here's what it translates to:

"F" stands for "fluorescent"

(European lamps begin with "TL")

"40" indicates the wattage

"T12" indicates the diameter of the tube in 8ths of an inch, or about an inch and a half in this case, and

"50U" is an abbreviation for the lamp type, in this case, Phillips 5000K Ultralume™

Chapter Three
GADGETS AND GIZMOS

Let's review. A saltwater set-up differs from a freshwater set-up primarily in the level of attention that the aquarist should pay to the selection of filtration and lighting systems. This is because marine organisms are less forgiving of inappropriate environmental conditions than are their freshwater counterparts. Aside from these two components, the equipment for a marine tank is identical to that for a freshwater tank. Simple enough, but, oh, what a plethora of doo-dads and thing-ma-bobs there are for filtering and lighting a saltwater tank.

I stated in the last chapter that even the novice marine aquarist should consider a wet/dry filtration system, although good results can be obtained, with diligent effort, by the aquarist who uses an undergravel filter. But what about all that other hardware: protein skimmers, ultraviolet sterilizers, ozonizers, redox controllers, oxygen reactors, automatic dispensing devices, timers, wave makers, and so forth? And, regarding wet/dry filters, how do you choose among the many designs available? These questions must be answered at the outset. Once the aquarium is established, altering the equipment package can be costly and time-consuming, not to mention stressful for the tank's inhabitants.

Let's start with the add-on hardware. Each and every one of these devices has an appropriate application, but, with the exception of the protein skimmer, none should be considered "standard". In other words, any marine tank will benefit from the use of a protein skimmer, but not everyone needs all of the other stuff. Make no mistake, however, all of the other stuff is useful, provided you understand what each item is useful for.

Wet/Dry Filters

Wet/dry filters? They all do pretty much the same thing, but there are good designs and poor ones. Choosing a wet/dry filter is much like choosing a car. Any old clunker will get you to the office and back home again, but a Mercedes provides a better ride, less frequent maintenance, and generally a better design than, say, a reconditioned Ford Pinto. My Dad, whose first car was a Model T, thought I was foolish to spend the extra money for power mirrors on my current car, but even he admits this is a great convenience when you need to adjust the mirror on the passenger's side while driving on the interstate at rush hour. With a wet/dry filter, you are spending money to obtain a good design; a filter that merely accomplishes biological filtration is the aquarium equivalent of a reconditioned Pinto. Look for the following design features in a wet/dry filter:

• **a biological chamber that will hold sufficient media for the size tank you have.**

Most filters use media made of molded plastic in various shapes and colors. You will generally need about a gallon of these plastic widgets for each 25 gallons of water in the tank.

• **a warranty against leakage, the longer the better.**

• **a "drip tray" at the top of the biological chamber, to distribute the water from the tank evenly over the filter media.**

A rotating spray bar is sometimes used to insure even water distribution. This component will succumb to friction and stop rotating sooner or later, while a drip tray is nearly fail-safe. Score extra points for the design if the tray is part of a drawer that can be easily pulled out for access. You will place a layer of polyester fiber pad over the holes in the drip tray, to trap debris. This pad will need frequent cleaning and therefore must be easily accessible, without shutting down the entire system.

• **There should be a slanted plate underneath the biological chamber, to direct detritus toward the**

middle of the filter sump, where it can be easily removed.

• The sump should be roomy enough to accomodate additional equipment, such as a protein skimmer, and additional filtration media, such as activated carbon.

Score extra points if the filter comes with a built-in skimmer. Score a few extra points if there are handy compartments for other media. Make sure the aquarium cabinet is roomy enough, by the way, for the filter that you select. This seems like an obvious criterion, but I am always amazed at how often this key point is forgotten.

Most wet/dry filters are not supplied with a pump, and you should give careful attention to this important component. Select a pump that has a rated output of about five times the capacity of the tank. When in doubt, choose a larger pump, as too much water flow in a salt-water tank is seldom a problem, while too little flow can have serious consequences. Water pumps conform quite precisely to the old adage that says "you get what you pay for". Good pumps simply cost more than shoddy ones. Since the pump is the most important component of the filtration system, by all means buy a good one. Plumbing will be required to carry water from the tank to the filtration system, through the pump, and back to the tank. There are many possible designs for this plumbing, and the selection of individual parts will depend upon the size pipe needed, as well as the size of inlet and outlet holes in the filter and pump. Your best bet is to seek the assistance of the dealer from which you purchase the filtration system, and it is not a bad idea to carefully sketch out all the necessary connections before you purchase parts or begin to assemble the plumbing. Many systems now come with all the necessary plumbing. You can purchase the tank, filter, pump and plumbing parts as a kit. This is probably the wisest option for those aquarists who lack plumbing skills.

Now let us turn our attention to the additional equipment. Following is a brief explanation of what some of the most widely recommended devices can and cannot do, concluding with a more extended discussion of the protein skimmer, which, in my opinion, is a necessity.

Ultraviolet sterilizers

Ultraviolet sterilizers are simply enclosures that allow water to be pumped past a germicidal (UV) lamp. Exposure of the water to the UV radiation results in killing most, but not all, of the bacteria and protozoa that are suspended in the water. The term "sterilizer" is not quite correct, as most units can achieve only about a 98% "kill", so the water that leaves the sterilizer is not really sterile. This device is useful for multiple tank systems that share a common filter. Passing water from the filter through the sterilizer before it is returned to the tanks provides security against the transmission of disease from tank to tank. In this way, a problem that develops in one tank will not rapidly spread to every tank in the system. Using UV on a single tank provides a measure of protection from disease; if an infestation of parasites does develop, it cannot spread as rapidly as would be the case without the UV. In my view, the main drawback to using a UV device is that it tends to create a false sense of security on the part of the aquarist: if the sterilizer is working, basic maintenance can perhaps be neglected, and no harm will come to the fish. This is a very risky attitude. In addition, UV equipment requires regular and thorough maintenance. The lamps, which are expensive, must be replaced about every six months. The unit must also be cleaned, usually monthly, because the accumulation of slime, etc. on the glass sleeve that protects the lamp will quickly reduce the penetration of the UV radiation into the water, and thus lower the unit's effectiveness. If you are planning a tank that contains both fish and invertebrates, and which will be heavily stocked with live rock or other decorations that would make it difficult, or perhaps impossible, to catch and remove a fish for treatement should disease occur, a UV sterilizer may prove useful if it is properly maintained.

Ozonizers and redox controllers

Some aquarists who maintain reef tanks swear by these devices. Ozonizers are used to inject ozone, a highly reactive form of oxygen gas, into the aquarium water. The ozone oxidizes organic matter, which is a desirable function in any marine tank. Use of ozone will make it much easier to control undesirable algae growth, and many very desirable species of marine fishes appreciate the improved water quality that can be achieved with ozone use. Ozone also kills bacteria, and possibly, protozoan parasites.

The problem is that too much ozone can be very harmful to the tank's inhabitants, and the wise aquarist will not use it unless the ozonizer is controlled by a redox controller. This is an electronic device that controls the ozonizer in much the same way that a thermostat controls a furnace, regulating the introduction of ozone into the system so that just enough, but not too much, is added. An ozonizer and redox controller, together with a good air pump, ozone resistant airline tubing (ordinary airline tubing is rapidly destroyed by ozone), and an ozone resistant check valve (which prevents water from entering the ozonizer and creating a shock hazard), will set you back a bit, financially. If you are willing to make the investment, this equipment is a good idea; however, do not be lulled into thinking, as mentioned above for UV equipment, that all will be well as long as the ozonizer and controller are working properly. If you are a beginner contemplating a fish-only tank, this equipment is not necessary. You will be better off, in the long run, to learn more about your aquarium before you invest in such high-tech hardware. If your first tank is to be a reef tank, consider ozone a desirable, but not required, option.

Wave makers

As I stated in my first book, *The Reef Tank Owner's Manual*, wave makers are a nifty, but not necessary, idea. Basically, a wave maker is an electronic timer that allows you to switch alternately between two powerheads placed in the tank, simulating the surge and flow of tidal currents that would be found on a natural reef. This effect is important for sessile invertebrates, and is clearly enjoyed by certain fishes, but you can certainly get along without it. If you select a system pump with sufficiently high capacity, consider using return plumbing that provides more than one outlet. One pump can thus be used to create two or more jets of water at different locations in the tank. Having multiple return outlets creates more turbulence than a single outlet.

Automatic dispensing devices

There are several designs for automatic dispensing devices. All of them accomplish the same thing:

adding small amounts of water or tank additives on a regular, programmed basis. For reef tank owners, such equipment is usually used to add water to make up for evaporation losses, and to add calcium supplements, which are important for long term survival of corals and other invertebrates that extract calcium from the water. Obviously, you can do these chores manually, if you are conscientious. Consider automated equipment if you are the sort of person that never remembers to have the air conditioner serviced until the middle of August.

I do advocate installation of a device that automatically adds water to the aquarium to compensate for evaporation. In the summertime (at least in the Sunbelt, where I live) adding water to the tank can be a daily chore, because air conditioning lowers the humidity inside the home or office. Humidity is only one of the many factors that affect the rate of water loss by evaporation from the aquarium. Since many of these factors cannot be easily controlled, it is impossible to predict how much water a particular tank may lose in a given period of time. This is why automatic replacement of evaporated water is so desirable. For a modest amount, you can buy an all-plastic valve that will allow water from a reservoir (anything from a plastic Coke bottle to a five-gallon bucket) to drip into the tank by gravity each time the aquarium water level falls below a certain point. This saves time, and the salinity of the tank thus remains very stable. This is good for the tank's inhabitants, and spares the hassle of checking the tank each morning before you venture forth to brave the free-way. Remember that only water leaves the tank by evaporation. Therefore, use *only* purified water (dis-tilled or reverse osmosis) for evaporation replacement.

Reactors

Reef tank enthusiasts sometimes employ various "reactors" to increase the levels of dissolved gases in the aquarium water, oxygen, carbon dioxide, and ozone, most commonly. These devices work very well, but only some tanks need the extra help. Install such equipment only if there are problems that, based on water analysis, can be traced to an insufficiency of dissolved gases. Most tanks do not need this kind of assistance.

Timers

Use a timer to control the tank lights, creating a consistent day-night cycle of 10 - 12 hours of light and 14 - 12 hours of darkness automatically. Otherwise, flip the switch on the light fixture on a regular sched-ule. (By the way, some aquarium light fixtures require modification in order for them to work with a timer. This is because aquarium light fixture manufacturers may supply an outmoded "preheat" ballast, which is less desirable than a "rapid start" ballast. If your fixture has a rapid start ballast, you can use a timer without modi-fying the fixture. If you need to modify the fixture, consult an electrician; it's relatively easy and inexpensive to do.)

In summary, I suggest you carefully weigh the benefits to be derived from the equipment just described, versus the cost involved, before you buy. Read some of the advanced literature on the application of such equipment, and then decide what is right for you. Write me, if you need additional help, but, please, do some reading first.

Protein Skimmers

Do, however, buy yourself a protein skimmer. Protein skimmers do not remove only proteins from the water, they remove a lot of other unnecessary junk, as well. All skimmers work on the same principle. Tank water is mixed with very fine air bubbles, creating foam within the skimmer. Proteins and other organic matter dissolved in the water tends to collect on the surface of the bubbles of foam. As the foam builds up, it rises to the top of the skimmer, spilling over into a collection cup, and eventually filling the cup with a greenish brown goo that can be periodically dumped out. I have yet to see a marine aquarium that was not improved by the use of a skimmer. In fact, many reef tanks, including my own, are now filtered exclusively with this device (along with plenty of good quality live rock). A skimmer for a small tank can cost under $20; a good skimmer for a larger tank can cost over $300. When choosing a skimmer, bear in mind that you will pay for two features: 1) A skimmer that can be hidden away, rather than taking up room in the tank itself, will cost more, since such an external skimmer must be leak-proof. 2) A skimmer that uses a venturi valve to create the air/water mix will cost more than one that uses an air pump and air diffusers to achieve the same result. Venturi-type skimmers offer the advantage of relatively little maintenance, compared to air-operated types, which need new airstones every 3 or 4 weeks.

Much has been written about choosing an appropriate skimmer, and I will not attempt to summarize all of this information here. My experience has been that the recommendations made by skimmer manufacturers, regarding the size tank for which the skimmer is appropriate, are generally reliable. There are hundreds of skimmers from which to choose. When in doubt, buy the larger model. It is not possible to "over-skim" the aquarium. Even a small, inefficient skimmer is better than none at all. Just make sure that you understand how to install and operate the skimmer properly.

The skimmer should be adjusted so that a relatively small amount of rather "dry" foam collects in the cup. It make take a few days, and a bit of fiddling with the air supply (or flow rate, if it is a venturi skimmer) to achieve the desired result. The exact adjustment will vary from one tank to another. Most beginners adjust the air supply or flow rate too high, so that water, not foam, collects in the cup. Start with a setting that seems too low at first, and note how the foam builds up after a period of time has elapsed. It may take several hours for foam to begin collecting in the cup. With only a little experience, you will get the hang of it. If your tank is quite new, very little foam may collect, as there will be only a small amount of material present for the skimmer to remove. This does not indicate that something is wrong with the skimmer, only that the water does not contain much organic matter, which is a desirable condition. Get yourself a skimmer, fiddle with it a bit, and keep all that organic junk from making life hard for your fish and/or invertebrates.

Chapter Four
WATER
CHEMISTRY

Don't be afraid of that title. I am not going to delve into the esoterica of marine water chemistry, as this is a discipline best left to graduate schools, oceanographic institutes, and, perhaps, a few advanced aquarium hobbyists. I will, rather, explain what every marine aquarist absolutely, positively must learn and understand about testing the water in his/her tank, and how to interpret the test results.

Water Tests

For starters, all brands of water tests are not created equal. I have found only a few widely available brands that are truly satisfactory. The others I have tried are either inaccurate, difficult to read, or both. Suffice it to say that there is little point in buying tests that are inaccurate, as obtaining faulty information about the chemistry of your tank is really worse than obtaining no information at all.

Marine aquarists (beginner or advanced) who intend to keep only fish will need the following tests:

- **ammonia**
- **nitrite**
- **nitrate**
- **pH**
- **alkalinity**
- **phosphate (maybe)**
- **copper (maybe)**

Aquarists who intend to keep invertebrates will need, in addition to those mentioned, tests for:

- **calcium**
- **phosphate (definitely)**
- **iron (maybe)**

Regardless of which test kits you buy, follow the instructions for their use precisely. Always rinse out test vials thoroughly with fresh water after each use, and then rise the vial with the water to be tested prior to each use. Do not store test reagents for more than a year.

Everyone will need, in addition to chemical tests, an accurate hydrometer and an accurate thermometer. The hydrometer and thermometer measure specific gravity and temperature, respectively. These two numbers are related, as you will soon see, and are of great importance to marine organisms.

Temperature Control

Thermometers are no doubt familiar to everyone, so we will not dwell on the subject of temperature measurement, except to say that marine organisms do best at temperatures within the range of about 70° to 80° F, with the optimum being 75°. It is important that the temperature does not fluctuate widely in the course of a day. Your tank's temperature will depend to some extent on how you heat and cool the room in which the tank is kept. If the room is rather warm during the day, and the tank temperature climbs to 79° routinely, then it is better to set the heater to keep the tank at 79° during the evening hours, rather than allow the temperature to drop to, say, 72°, after everyone goes to bed. I repeat, however, that the ideal temperature is 75°. If you plan on keeping invertebrates, and stony corals in particular (See Chapter Seven for more information on stony corals.), you *must* keep the temperature near 75° at all times. Further, the metabolic rate (the way in which the body obtains energy from foods) in marine fishes is highly dependent on temperature. Keeping marine fishes at the optimum temperature of 75° results in better health, faster growth and fewer disease problems than at higher temperatures. This may mean that a chiller is necessary for your aquarium. Since a chiller can represent a sizable investment, it is prudent for you to understand how a chiller works, and what features you should look for when purchasing one.

An aquarium chiller (also called a "fluid chiller") operates in essentially the same manner as your refrigerator or air conditioner. A refrigerant gas, commonly Freon™ is compressed by an electrically driven compressor, which results in the gas losing energy, i.e., its temperature goes down. The compressed gas flows through a heat exchanger, where it picks up heat from the surrounding medium, in this case water from the aquarium that is being pumped through the exchanger. The gas carries this heat back toward the compressor, and on the way encounters an expansion valve, which allows the gas pressure to drop. As the pressure drops, the gas gives up heat to a radiator, which, in turn, dispels the heat into the surrounding air with the aid of a fan. This is a relatively simple process to describe, but actually building a refrigeration unit requires considerable precision in the machine shop.

From the foregoing discussion it can be seen that a chiller does not "create cold". Rather, it removes heat from the aquarium water. The rate at which a particular chiller removes heat determines its efficiency. Heat is measured in BTU's (British Thermal Units). One BTU is the amount of heat required to raise the temperature of one pound of water by $1°F$. Thus, the higher the BTU rating of the chiller, the faster it will lower the temperature of a tank of given size. This means, in practice, that a chiller with a high BTU rating will keep the tank at a constant temperature with less use of electricity and less wear and tear on the compressor than will a chiller of lower BTU rating. Unfortunately, often a particular chiller's BTU rating can only be determined in actual use of the chiller, which is seldom practical if you are merely considering a purchase. Your dealer, or a chiller manufacturer, may be of help in this regard.

There are some aspects of chiller design that you can look for, however. For example, the physical arrangement of the chiller components can be important. The heat exchanger and compressor must be in a fixed position relative to each other. This means that chillers with a flexible connection between the exchanger and compressor are a poor choice. (If the exchanger is placed above the compressor, the exchanger will be "starved" for refrigerant gas; if lower than the compressor, the exchanger will be "flooded", assuming they were designed to operate on the same level originally.)

In addition, the choice of material for the heat exchanger is important. Remember that the purpose of the heat exchanger is to gather heat from the water. This means that as much exchanger surface as possible must be brought into contact with the water in a given period of time. Chillers using exchangers composed of the metal titanium, for example, generally have smaller, less efficient exchangers. This is because titanium is intrinsically expensive, is difficult to machine, and is a poor conductor of heat similar to stainless steel. Titanium is used for marine tank chillers primarily because it is one of the few affordable metals that is impervious to seawater. (Gold or platinum would do, of course, but ...) A more satisfactory exchanger for marine tank use can be made of copper tubing sheathed with a plastic such as Teflon™. This material is relatively cheap, and is impervious to seawater. Also, copper is the best conductor of heat known (except for sterling silver, another impractical choice).

In summary, you will need a chiller if your aquarium does not remain close to 75°F throughout the year, especially for invertebrates, but also for the healthiest fishes. Chiller designs can vary widely and there are a number of factors that one must carefully consider before choosing one. The most efficient chiller designs will have a high BTU rating, but this information may not be readily available for aquarium chillers (it is *required* for home refrigerators and air conditioners, by Federal law). Do your homework and choose your chiller wisely.

Specific Gravity

Measuring the specific gravity of the tank allows one to estimate the salinity of the water, if the temperature is known. "Salinity" refers to the amount of dissolved solids (salts) in the water, and, in a typical sample of ocean water is 3.5% or 35 parts per thousand (ppt). For water of a given salinity, the specific gravity reading varies with the temperature. At 75°, the specific gravity of water at a salinity of 35 ppt is 1.0240. Although many authorities suggest that a lower specific gravity (usually 1.0220) is OK, I prefer to imitate Mother Nature, and keep my tanks at 1.0240.

Water Chemistry

Water Itself

Strangely, aquarists do not often give thought to the quality of the fresh water that they use to prepare synthetic seawater, and most use plain tap water. I would recommend strongly against this, as, unfortunately, municipal tap water and well waters are frequently unsatisfactory for aquarium use. This is due to the presence of pollutants that, while not deemed harmful for drinking purposes, can cause problems in the marine aquarium. Algae nutrients such as phosphate and silica, toxic metals such as copper, and a host of other compounds may all be found in "pure" tap water. I recommend that all water used for the marine tank be purified in some way.

For hobbyists with low water needs, the best bet may be to purchase distilled water at the grocery store. If you need significant amounts of purified water, however, it is much cheaper in the long run to purify tap water via reverse osmosis (RO). This technique uses water pressure to force tap water through a special membrane, in effect "straining out" pollutants and producing, in most practical applications, water that is about 90% free of contaminants. RO units have two drawbacks. Water is produced drop by drop, with typical units producing about 25 gallons of water per day, so a reservoir is needed. Also, about four gallons of waste water are produced for every gallon of product water. The waste water can be used for cleaning or irrigation purposes, however.

If the tap water is very contaminated, some troublesome compounds, such as phosphate, for example, may remain in the product water in an amount sufficient to cause problems in the aquarium. If this turns out to be the case in your community, RO water may need further purification by the use of deionization. This technique involves the use of special chemical resins to absorb undesired components from the water. The addition of a deionization filter to an RO system can result in purified water comparable to glass distilled water. Deionization can also be used as the sole means of water purification, dispensing with RO altogether, but this is a more expensive option, as the special resins must be periodically replaced, and they are costly. The advantages of using deionization alone are that water is produced on demand, not dropwise, and there is no waste water production.

Nitrogen Compounds

Ammonia, nitrite, and nitrate are components of the biological filtration process. Proteins, found in every kind of food that might be eaten by a fish or an invertebrate, contain amino compounds. These eventually wind up in one of two places, in the proteins of the animal that consumed the food, or in the water, as excreted ammonia. As you might expect, fish and invertebrates do not thrive if forced to live in their own excreta. Fortunately, nitrifying bacteria can be cultivated in the aquarium's filtration system, and these will convert the toxic ammonia first into nitrite and then into nitrate. Tests for ammonia and nitrite are used to determine if the important process of biological filtration is proceeding correctly. Tests for each of these compounds should always be zero.

Nitrate, the primary end product of biological filtration, may be tolerated, with the degree of tolerance varying with the nature of the organism. Some species of fish, groupers for example, can tolerate concentrations of nitrate in excess of 100 parts per million (ppm). Tangs and angels, on the other hand, may refuse to eat if the nitrate ion concentration exceeds 40 ppm. Most invertebrates are intolerant of nitrates, although hermit crabs seem indifferent to nitrate concentration, and giant clams actually remove nitrates from the water. You should test your tank for nitrate on a weekly basis, and carry out water changes often enough to keep the nitrate concentration low enough to suit the organisms in the tank. When in doubt, strive for a concentration of nitrate ion of less than 40 ppm for fish-only aquariums, and less than 10 ppm for tanks with invertebrates. If you want to avoid excessive algae growth, strive for the lowest possible nitrate concentration. It has been suggested that nitrate itself is not the culprit, but rather that the accumulation (or perhaps depletion) of other compounds as the result of too infrequent a schedule of water changes may be responsible for the harmful effects attributed to nitrate. This is most likely the case, as laboratory studies have shown that nitrate is not toxic to many kinds of marine life. Nevertheless, the measurement of nitrate accumulation can be used by the aquarist as an indicator of the need to perform a partial water change. It does little harm, in my view, to *think* of nitrate accumulation as harmful, even though this is not strictly correct. The point is that the condition of aquarium water changes over time, that these changes are generally undesirable, and that they can be alleviated via partial water changes.

pH

The degree of acidity or alkalinity of the aquarium water is measured as pH. Seawater is alkaline, and has a pH of 8.3. As acid is added to seawater the pH drops, with the minimum acceptable reading being about 7.8 or so. Acid is a byproduct of the biological filtration process referred to above. In addition, when carbon dioxide is released into the water as a result of respiration by fishes or invertebrates, it reacts with water to produce carbonic acid. Thus, the tendency in any aquarium is toward a *decline* in pH. Maintaining the correct pH can be accomplished by regular water changes, or through the addition of buffering agents designed to increase and stabilize the pH. Bicarbonate of soda is a common component of many of these formulations. Pay special attention to pH, and alkalin-

TABLE 4-1
Recommended Water Parameters

Parameter	Optimum	Test
Temperature	75°F	Daily
Salinity	35 ppt	See text
Ammonia	Zero	P
Nitrite	Zero	P
Nitrate	10 - 40 ppm	Weekly
pH	8.2 - 8.3	Weekly
Alkalinity	2.5 - 3.5 meq/l	Weekly
Calcium	400 ppm	Weekly
Phosphate	Undetectable	Weekly
Iron	0.05 - 0.10 ppm	*
Strontium	8 ppm	**
Iodine	1 ppm	**

P = Test when a problem is suspected; * = Important only for seaweed culture; ** = Test not available

ity, mentioned below, if yours is a fish-only aquarium. I will explain why in a moment.

Alkalinity

Alkalinity (which is often referred to as "buffer capacity", "KH" or "carbonate hardness") is a measure of the *resistance of the water to a change in pH as acid is added*. It is expressed in units called "milliequivalents per liter" (meq/l) and should be maintained at about 3.5 meq/l or above. (Higher is much better than lower.) If the alkalinity of the tank is high, it will be easier for the correct pH to be maintained.

This is important to the respiration of your fishes. Marine fishes depend, as do you and I, upon a specialized pigment, hemoglobin, in their blood to carry oxygen to their body tissues. However, there is no special carrier for carbon dioxide, a toxic byproduct of respiration. This poisonous gas must escape from the fish's body directly into the water, and the rate at which it leaves the fish is determined in part by the amount of carbon dioxide already present in the water surrounding the fish. Fortunately, in seawater of sufficiently high alkalinity, carbon dioxide is converted to the harmless bicarbonate ion, and all is well. However, as the alkalinity of the aquarium becomes "used up" carbon dioxide can accumulate in the water, making it increasingly difficult for the fish to eliminate this gas from its body. In consequence, therefore, carbon dioxide begins to accumulate in the fish's blood. When this happens, the fish's body chemistry swings into action, and the carbon dioxide in its bloodstream is converted, again into harmless bicarbonate ions. Unfortunately, the fish cannot cope with this situation indefinitely, and its blood pH begins to decline. When this happens, the hemoglobin loses its ability to carry oxygen, and the fish suffocates, *despite the fact that there is abundant oxygen available!* I realize that this has been a long and rather complicated description of a chain of events. The point is, simply, that allowing the alkalinity of your aquarium to decline significantly may spell disaster for the tank's inhabitants. Interestingly, most invertebrates, which do not depend upon hemoglobin in their respiratory processes, are not so sensitive to pH and alkalinity levels. Invertebrates nevertheless fare better when these parameters are within the range they encounter in the ocean. Keep the pH of your tank at 8.3 and the alkalinity above 2.5 meq/l (equivalent to 7 dKH, or 125 ppm carbonate hardness). Test for this parameter every week. It can be adjusted by the additon of chemical powders made for the purpose, or by carrying out a partial water change. Note that different brands of test kits use different units for expressing this parameter. I have given the preferred readings in each of the most commonly used units.

Phosphate

You may or may not need to test for phosphate. Do so only if you have an annoying problem with undesirable, or excessive, algae growth, of if you plan to keep invertebrates such as anemones, which dislike phosphates. Phosphate concentrations above the limit of detection for most test kits (about 0.05 - 0.10 ppm) are often associated with algae "blooms" in the tank. Algae growth may range from a slimy film on the glass and decorations, to green water. Each aquarist has an opinion as to the amount of algae growth that is considered "desirable", as algae itself is not harmful. Indeed, many fishes, such as tangs and angelfishes, thrive if abundant green filamentous algae is available for them to nibble on all day long. Some invertebrates, on the other hand, can be suffocated if algae is allowed to grow on them. Suffice it to say that if you determine that you have an algae "problem", a phosphate test kit will be an important tool in dealing with it.

Copper

Problems, problems. No worthwhile pursuit is free from problems, and neither will your aquarium be. Sooner or later, you will have to deal with a case of saltwater "ich" (*Cryptocaryon*) or of "coral fish disease" (*Amyloodinium*), if you keep saltwater fish. Even if you are an accomplished aquarist, one day the electricity will be off at your house for many hours, or your toddler will "help" Daddy by feeding the fish an entire can of food, and despite your best efforts, one or more fish will develop one or both of these annoying parasite problems. I will discuss in more detail the diagnosis and treatment of these two nusianccs in Chapter Eight. For now, suffice it to say that the most reliable, effective treatment for a fish infected with either of these microscopic parasites is to add copper ions to the water. To do this correctly, you will need a copper test kit (and, ideally, a spare "hospital" tank). May as well buy both now, so you will be prepared for the inevitable. ·

Calcium

If you are going to keep invertebratcs that require large amounts of calcium for the construction of their   shells, skeletons, carapaces, or what have you, you will need to monitor the calcium concentration of the aquarium water. Corals, soft corals, clams, snails, scallops, crabs, starfish, sea urchins, and even some algae, extract calcium from the water continuously. Seawater contains about 400 ppm of calcium. Some seawater mixes provide only about half this amount. Adding a calcium supplement, in amounts determined by testing the water for calcium on a regular basis, is important for these animals. Even for fish-only tanks, however, it is wise to keep the calcium con-centration at natural seawater level.

Iron

Seaweeds ("macroalgae") require iron, as do the microscopic algae that live in the bodies of certain invertebrates (anemones, corals, giant clams, etc.) You will need to add an iron supplement to the water, again, based on the results of an iron test kit, however, only if you intend to cultivate lots of macroalgae. Fish, and many kinds of invertebrates, are indifferent to the iron concentration, and need only small amounts that cannot be measured with hobbyist equipment.

I have summarized all of the foregoing in Table II. This has been a discussion of "cookbook" aquarium chemistry. The details, rationale, etc., would fill vol-umes. The numbers I have given above are the best available to me, and are based on experience as well as extensive reading on the subject. I can only empha-size that you should buy good test kits, use them on a regular basis, and keep a written record of the results. Record the following information about your tank in a log book. This is the single, most important aspect of good aquarium maintenance:

- **date**
- **test(s) performed and results**

- **chemicals added and amounts**
- **temperature**
- **specific gravity**
- **amount of water changed**
- **species and size of fish or other animals added**
- **incidents of death or disease, treatments and results**
- **any comments or observations you think pertinent**

Regular testing, good records, and consistent maintenance are the keys to a successful saltwater aquarium. Next, a discussion of what maintenance to perform consistently, and how to make maintenance chores as hassle-free as possible.

Chapter Five
ROUTINE MAINTENANCE

Aquarium-keeping is a lot like housekeeping. Some of the nicest people I know are consistently untidy, and some of the nattiest, everything-in-its-place housekeepers leave a lot to be desired as social or business acquaintances. In other words, a "clean" aquarium does not necessarily imply that the inhabitants are thriving. And a "dirty" tank may not be a really unhealthy environment for fish or invertebrates. Nevertheless, routine maintenance duties are an essential part of marine aquarium keeping. Do not make the common mistake, however, of constantly "fiddling" with the tank. Develop a maintenance program that places minimum demands upon your busy schedule, and, above all, stick to it. Regular, appropriate maintenance will make the difference between having a marine tank that is a pleasure to own, and having continual problems. Let's structure an aquarium maintenance plan with a checklist, and elaborate upon some specific chores. Notice that the nature of the inhabitants of the tank is taken into account. Bear in mind that one of the most important aspects of aquarium maintenance is consistency. Feel free to modify the checklist that follows to suit your lifestyle. Just make sure that, whatever routine you choose, you stick with it.

FISH-ONLY AQUARIUMS
Daily Maintenance

• **Feed fish once or twice, choosing with care both the type and amount of food.**

Give each of your fishes a quick health check. Is each one behaving in the normal manner for its species? Most fish should feed eagerly, and have clear, bright colors and alert behavior. Some experience in observing healthy fishes will help you to judge the condition of your tank's inhabitants. Of course, if something is amiss, take prompt action.

• **Note the temperature of the tank, and check to see if fresh water should be added to compensate for evaporation.**

Adjust the heater and add fresh water as needed. Distilled water or reverse osmosis water is preferable to tap water for this purpose. Always replace evaporated water frequently enough that you do not have to add more than a quart or two per ten gallons of tank water. Some aquarists simply add a little fresh water every day, after experience has taught them how much to add, on average.

• **Quickly check out all the equipment to see that everything is working properly.**

Take corrective action, or make a note to do so later, if needed.

Weekly Maintenance

• **Test and log results for specific gravity, nitrate, pH and alkalinity.**

Add a buffer compound, or change water, to correct pH and alkalinity. Consider changing water if the nitrate is beginning to get too high. Adjust the specific gravity, if necessary. Add fresh water if the specific gravity is too high. Add concentrated brine made from synthetic seawater mix (about one cup mix per one cup tap water) to raise the specific gravity, if needed.

• **Clean the front glass of the tank, inside and out.**

• **Inspect and clean the filter pad in the drip tray of your wet/dry filter.**

• **Siphon any accumulated detritus out of the tank, simultaneously remove about 10% percent of the water, and replace it with new synthetic seawater.**

Aquarists with wet/dry filters may opt to change water and remove detritus monthly, but I recommend a more frequent schedule of smaller amounts, rather than a larger, less frequent change. If you do decide on monthly changes, change 25%.

Monthly Maintenance

• **Change some water, as part of your regular schedule**

• **Siphon as much detritus as possible from the tank.**

If using an undergravel filter, use a siphon designed to "vacuum" the gravel bed to remove trapped debris.

• **Check the operation of all equipment.**

Empty the collection cup of the protein skimmer, and replace its airstone, if not using a venturi skimmer. Clean the UV sterilizer sleeve if you use this accessory.

Less than monthly maintenance

• **Follow the manufacturer's instructions for regular maintenance of equipment such as the pump, which may need oiling or other care from time to time.**

• **Change UV sterilizer lamps about every six months.**

• **Change the lamps in your light fixture at least once a year, unless you are using metal halide lamps, which maintain their brightness for several thousand hours.**

• **Every so often, you will need to do a BIG water change (50% or more) to lower the nitrate concentration of the tank.**

Since nitrate constantly accumulates, the trend will be for nitrate to increase, despite regular small water changes. Each tank is different in the rate at which nitrate builds up. You can determine easily, if you test regularly and keep records, when to do a major water change. Plan on at least twice a year.

TANKS WITH INVERTEBRATES

I am assuming that you do not have a "reef" tank, by which I mean a tank housing corals, anemones, and other light-requiring invertebrates. For an invertebrate tank that is not a reef tank, do the following, in addition to the maintenance recommended above:

Weekly Maintenance

Feed your invertebrates appropriately. Some types, such as feather dusters and sea cucumbers, need small, suspended particles of food to strain from the water. Live, newly hatched brine shrimp are ideal, but there are many good prepared foods available. Other invertebrates, such as shrimps and some mollusks, need larger food items. Follow specific recommendations for feeding each of the invertebrates that you keep. (I will provide some advice on feeding invertebrates in a later chapter.) Also, check and adjust the calcium concentration of the tank.

REEF TANKS

I define a reef tank as one in which invertebrates that require intense lighting are kept. If you have chosen to launch your aquarium venture with a reef tank, you should, in addition to all of the recommendations listed above, carry out the following maintenance procedures:

Weekly Maintenance

• **Test nitrate, phosphate and calcium.**

Adjust nitrate appropriately via a water change. Adjust calcium by the addition of a calcium supplement, or by a water change.

• **Add a strontium supplement to the tank, if you wish.**

You cannot easily test for strontium, but it is required by corals and some other invertebrates that produce calcareous skeletons. Aquarists have reported enhanced growth of some of these organisms when strontium supplements are added.

Monthly Maintenance

• **Check for correct operation of any equipment, such as the ozonizer/redox controller system, if you are using one.**

• **Replace any specialized chemical filtration media that you may be using, such as activated carbon.**

The pros and cons of using chemical filtration media are outside the scope of this book. Suffice it to say that there are circumstances in which such media are desirable. Their application, however, must be judged on an individual, tank-by-tank basis.

SEAWATER PREPARATION AND STORAGE

If from the foregoing you derive the general impression that I advocate frequent partial water changes as the key to success with marine aquarium keeping, you are correct. Every marine aquarist should be prepared to carry out water changes whenever desirable. Always make certain that new seawater is similar to the tank in terms of its temperature, specific gravity, and pH before you add it to an established aquarium! Like chicken soup, synthetic seawater is always better if made the day before it is used. Have a suitable container of seawater on hand for carrying out water changes.

A clean, covered plastic trash can is ideal for storing seawater. If stored covered in a cool, dark place such as a garage, basement or closet, seawater keeps indefinitely, so it is easy to mix up a large amount to have available for water changes as needed. Choose a storage container suitable for food for storing seawater. A little more than two cups of seawater mix will make five gallons of seawater. Always use distilled or RO water for making synthetic seawater. Buy dry salt mix in large quantities to save on its cost. It keeps indefinitely if stored in a tightly sealed container away from moisture, which promotes caking. A common problem with stored seawater is that the storage temperature is much lower than the temperature of the tank. Here are two tips for solving this problem. Make a concentrated brine by dissolving the required amount of salt in only 2/3 as much water as you are going to need. When ready to use, add hot fresh water to the brine to dilute it to the correct specific gravity. Alternatively, prepare water to the desired specific gravity and store it. When ready to use, heat a portion of the water to the temperature of a cup of coffee using your microwave oven, and mix the heated water back into the cooler water to raise its temperature to that of the tank. *Note: Never heat seawater to the boiling point, and never heat it in a metal container.*

And that's about it. It took a lot of words to explain how to go about it, which may give the impression that proper maintenance requires a lot of time. In practice, the maintenance of your marine tank will require about five minutes every day, an additional half hour or so every week, and about an hour every month. Every so often, perhaps twice a year, you'll need to spend an afternoon on a really thorough job of care.

This chapter concludes our discussion of the basics of marine aquarium keeping. The maintenance procedures I have recommended should become routine to you, regardless of the nature of the fishes and/or invertebrates that you keep. Each of the 1500 or so species of living organisms available in the marine aquarium trade, however, has its own special needs. Understanding the specialized requirements of each of the species that you place in your marine aquarium should be your goal, after having mastered the basics of good aquarium care. In the next chapter, I will cover the needs of twenty of the most popular and hardy marine fish species. These examples will be chosen to be representative of the array of species that you may see. I can, at best, only provide the briefest of introductions to the world of marine fishes, however. Why not begin some additional reading now, to provide yourself with some background familiarity about the fishes you may plan to keep? There are many books on marine fishes, any of which may be helpful in regard to one species or another. If you want an exhaustive treatise on the subject, replete with lots of color pictures, I recommend the *Atlas of Marine Aquarium Fishes*, by Dr. Warren Burgess, published by TFH Publications, Neptune, New Jersey. There are also a number of specialized books on marine fishes; these generally cover the species found in a particular area of the world, and often may not have specific information about aquarium care. They are, nevertheless, quite useful. Remember to read, learn and plan *before* you buy any living creature for your marine aquarium.

Chapter Six
SUMMARY OF MARINE FISH FAMILIES

Most of the fishes in this chapter will fare quite well in the typical marine tank. Therefore, before launching into a description of common marine fish families, I thought it would be wise to define what I mean by a "typical" marine aquarium set-up.

While no two tanks are alike, it is possible to describe an aquarium that reflects, on average, what the majority of marine aquarists actually buy. For a fish-only aquarium, most people set up a 30-75 gallon tank, outfitted with an undergravel filter operated by powerheads, and an external power or cannister filter containing activated carbon. Wet/dry filters are becoming more popular for this type of tank, and I recommend this approach to the beginner. Light is supplied by a single fluorescent lamp. Before animals are added to any marine tank, the biological filter must be established by one of a variety of methods. At the conclusion of this process, the aquarist performs a large water change, and checks pH, temperature, specific gravity, and nitrates. If all of these tests are found to be acceptable, specimens are added. If your aquarium is outfitted like this, and if water parameters are within acceptable limits, you are ready to add fish. If you intend to add invertebrates, with or without fish also, you should first read the introduction to the next chapter before you proceed with stocking your tank, even though it is generally a good idea to add fishes to a mixed community tank before invertebrates are added.

There are several hundred kinds of fishes and invertebrates regularly available in the aquarium trade. How is one to make sense of so wide a variety? One simple approach with fishes is to study the various *families*, rather than attempt to sort out the bewildering variety of individual species. Within a given family of fishes, reproductive behavior, feeding preferences, temperment, and other characteristics are relatively consistent. Thus, if one knows the general characteristics of the triggerfish family, for example, one will know what to expect of the Pinktail Triggerfish, with a fair degree of accuracy. There will always be exceptions, of course, and reference books should be checked when considering an unfamiliar, rare, or particularly expensive specimen. The experiences of other aquarists should also be sought out. The important point is to know what the fish requires in its natural habitat, and be certain you can provide for these requirements in the aquarium. Big fish obviously cannot go in a small tank, but the situation may be less obvious than this. For example, the Strawberry Basslet will not tolerate another of its kind within sight. Unless the aquarium is huge, two of these fish cannot be kept together.

What follows is not a complete guide to marine fishes, by any means. However, the information provided here should help you to begin the process of choosing fishes to keep in your tank. For color photographs and a brief descriptive note about virtually every species of marine fish that you are likely to encounter, consult Dr. Warren Burgess's *Atlas of Marine Aquarium Fishes*, published by TFH Publications. This book contains over 4000 color photos, and a series of symbols under each photo gives information on feeding, lighting, temperment, size, etc. Also consult other books devoted to fishes.

Not all families are listed below, only the ones that are the most popular and commonly available. For each family, a representative species is described.

• DAMSELFISHES

The many species of damselfishes may be considered as comprising three distinct groups:

a. Damsels -- Territorial, non-schooling fishes that are often agressive toward their tankmates, especially if the damsel fish is well-established in the tank. They are hardy, easy to feed, and tolerant of poor water conditions.

Blue Devil - *Chrysiptera cyanea* is a popular species. This species is solid blue; males from some localities have a yellow or orange tail. Females are blue with a small black dot at the posterior base of the dorsal fin. Keep one male and several females together in a thirty gallon tank.

b. Chromis -- These are schooling, peaceful damsels that feed on plankton. Hardy and undemanding, chromis are seldom aggressive. They must be kept in groups of three or more, as they fare poorly without companionship. A school of five could be housed comfortably in a thirty gallon tank.

Green Chromis - *Chromis viridis* is seafoam green in color, with a deeply forked tail. It shows off its colors to best advantage under bright illumination.

c. Clownfishes -- These are damselfishes specialized for living in symbiotic association with certain species of large sea anemones, and are often called anemonefishes. They can be kept without an anemone, but do better if the appropriate anemone is present. In this latter case, water conditions and lighting *conducive to the growth of the anemone* are most important. Highly territorial and defensive of the anemone, different species of adult clownfishes seldom tolerate each other in the aquarium. Much has been written on this popular and fascinating group.

Common Clownfish -- *Amphiprion ocellaris* is bright orange in color with three white vertical bars. Often the white bars are edged in black, but this is variable. Keep singly, in pairs or in a small group of juveniles. Different species of clownfishes have differing preferences in anemones, so it is wise to purchase the fish and anemone together, if possible. Unfortunately, the Common Clownfish prefers the anemone *Heteractis magnifica* , which is among the more difficult of anemones to keep successfully. Beginners are advised to keep the Common Clown without an anemone. If you *must* have the clown and anemone together, first read the next chapter. Also consult *Field Guide to the Anemonefishes and Their Anemones* , by Dr. Daphne Fautin and Dr. Gerald Allen, published by the Western Australian Museum, Perth, Western Australia (160 pages with color illustrations and photographs). I suggest you set up a thirty to fifty gallon tank with proper filtration and lighting for the anemone. Add one anemone of the appropriate species and a juvenile pair of clownfishes (hatchery-produced, if possible). Add no other fishes, and no other member of the coelenterate phylum (see next chapter). Decorate the tank with live rock, or use dead coral rock, shells, plastic coral reproductions, and/or plastic seaweed reproductions for decoration. Tankmates might include a variety of other invertebrates.

• TANGS

The popular tangs are all largely vegetarian fishes that live in large schools and cruise along the reef nibbling at algae. They are intolerant of nitrates above about 40 ppm (ion), and thus regular water changes are important. Feed frequently, providing vegetable matter such as lettuce or spinach upon which they can graze during the day. Also include other green foods, such as frozen seaweed, in the diet. Small amounts of meaty foods (worms, brine shrimp, etc.) will also be eaten, but should not be fed exclusively. Keep tangs in groups, or as individuals. The various species usually tolerate each other quite well, provided the tank is roomy. Choose a tank at least four feet in length, to provide plenty of swimming room. A fifty gallon tank could accommodate a "school" of three individuals.

Yellow Tang -- *Zebrasoma flavescens* is solid lemon yellow in color, hardy, inexpensive and popular.

• BIG PREDATORS

This designation includes several families. All grow rather large, and all are aggressively predatory toward tankmates small enough to be eaten. Good choices for a large tank, most of the fishes in this assortment are very hardy and long lived in the aquarium. All predators seem to be quite intelligent, and can become quite tame, even recognizing the aquarist that feeds them. Generally, feed such fishes every two or three days, and offer a variety of meaty seafoods. Live freshwater fishes will be eaten readily, but these should not form the staple diet, as freshwater fishes lack essential fatty acids that are required by marine predators. Feed mostly fresh or frozen marine fish meat, shrimp, shellfish and other, similar foods. This group includes:

a. Lionfishes -- All lionfishes are capable of inflicting a painful sting, so handle them with caution. Adult size ranges from the rare, 4-inch-long Fu Manchu lion, *Dendrochirus biocellatus*, to the Black Volitans

Lion, *Pterois lunulata*, at over 2 feet. Lionfishes tolerate each other well, and will not harm other fish that are
too large to eat.

Red Volitans Lion -- *P. volitans* is a common, large
species. It can live to be over fifteen years old in the
aquarium.

b. Groupers -- These fishes like to hide in am-
bush, waiting for prey. Most grow very large and are
popular food and sport fishes. Easy to keep, groupers
will eat almost anything small enough to swallow.

Panther Grouper -- *Chromileptes altivelis* is solid
white with black polka dots. Provide it with a roomy
tank, as a 3-inch baby can grow into a six-pound specimen in a few years time.

c. Moray Eels -- Moray eels are nearly blind, and
hunt by smell at night. They generally spend the day in
a hole or crevice, with just the head protruding. Most
get quite large, and some are aggressive, capable of
delivering a nasty bite.

Snowflake Moray -- *Echidna nebulosa.* rarely
grows larger than three feet, and is a peaceful and hardy
aquarium inhabitant. It is chocolate brown with cream
colored "snowflake" patterns on the body.

• TRIGGERFISHES

Triggerfishes, like the foregoing groups, are large,
hardy and aggressive. Generally intolerant of their own
kind in the aquarium, different species of triggers can
be kept together in a roomy tank if specimens are cho-

sen with care. They are intelligent, have powerful jaws, and may rearrange the tank decorations from time to time. Feed triggers a wide variety of meaty seafoods, as they will consume almost anything edible.

Clown Trigger -- *Balistoides conspicillum*, is beautifully patterned in black and yellow, with white polka dots. Although expensive, this is a very desirable aquarium species that will live for many years. Large individuals are sometimes aggressive toward tankmates for no apparent reason, so you may want to limit yourself to one Clown Trigger in a 75 gallon tank. Under such circumstances, and with patience and attention on your part, this fish will become a friendly pet that eats from your fingers, and recognizes your approach.

• ANGELFISHES

Angelfishes are found exclusively on coral reefs, and thus demand good water quality and a nutritious, varied diet high in vegetable matter. They fall into two groups:

a. Dwarf angels -- Rarely exceeding four inches in length, these beautiful fishes are ideal for a small tank. Provide them with plenty of hiding places, and do not attempt to mix different kinds together, as they may not get along. If small individuals are chosen and placed in a roomy tank all at one time, you can keep a harem of dwarf angels together. All start life as females, and later develop into males as they grow larger. This pattern will be repeated in the aquarium if you are patient.

Flame Angel -- *Centropyge loriculus* is found in deep water and feeds on a variety of seaweeds and invertebrates. It is bright red in color with markings in orange, blue and black. A less expensive choice is the Coral Beauty -- *Centropyge bispinnosus*, which is strikingly colored in orange and blue. Specimens from Australia have more orange on the body.

b. Large angels -- In these species, which in some cases may reach two feet in length, the juveniles are always different in color from the adults. Generally, juvenile specimens adapt better to aquarium life, and will change into their adult coloration when they reach an appropriate size. In the aquarium, the large angels are very demanding, and some species cannot be successfully kept under any circumstances. Since large angels often cost $100 or more, choose carefully and make sure you can provide the fish with what it needs to survive.

Queen Angel -- *Holacanthus ciliaris* from Florida and the Caribbean is considered by some to be the most beautiful of all fishes, with gaudy markings in yellow and blue. From the Indo-Pacific, the beautiful blue, black and white juveniles of the Koran Angelfish, *Pomacanthus semicirculatus*, are commonly available, and adapt well to aquarium life. Provide all large angelfishes with an aquarium of at least 75 gallons.

• BUTTERFLYFISHES

This family, like the angelfish family to which it is related, is found only on coral reefs. Some readily adapt to aquarium life, while others are best left in the wild, generally because of specialized feeding requirements. Some butterflyfishes will eat only the living polyps of certain types of corals, for example. It is therefore important to make sure you can identify correctly any specimen in which you are interested, in order to determine its feeding preferences. Also, some species of butterflyfishes are always found in pairs and will not fare well singly, even if feeding is not a problem.

Longnose Butterfly -- *Forcipiger longirostris* is frequently imported from Hawaii. It is bright yellow, with a black face "mask", and has a long, pointed snout that it uses to pluck small tidbits from the reef. Since it feeds on a variety of foods in nature, this fish adapts well to aquarium foods. It can be successfully kept singly, in pairs or in groups. Choose a 30 gallon tank, at minimum, for any butterflyfish, a larger tank if possible.

• WRASSES

The usually gaudy wrasses are mostly elongated, active fishes, and are highly variable in both size and coloration. All are carnivorous, feeding on a variety of crustaceans, worms, small fishes and the like. Generally, wrasses are peaceful fishes, except toward anything small enough to eat, so beware of including small shrimps, for example, in a tank housing a wrasse. Wrasses have three life stages, designated female, male and supermale. Most often, supermales are collected for the aquarium trade. In nature a group of males and females will generally be dominated by a single supermale, which differes markedly in color and pattern from the "regular" male and female. You can keep wrasses in similarly composed groups in the aquarium, but two supermales in the same tank will not tolerate each other.

Paddlefin Wrasse -- *Thalassoma lucasanum* is from the Sea of Cortez. The supermale is a beautiful pink color with blue green head and fins, and a bright yellow "collar" behind the head. Juveniles, on the other hand, are striped in pink, yellow and brown, and are called "Mexican Rock Wrasse". Juveniles will change into supermales in the aquarium, in some cases.

As a general rule, species from the foregoing groups are suitable for aquariums of fifty gallons or larger, and, with some exceptions, are not suitable tankmates for aquariums that feature invertebrates. For smaller tanks, or those that have many invertebrate specimens, damselfishes, some dwarf angels, and some smaller wrasses may be suitable, if species are chosen judiciously. From the groups described below, however, virtually all species may be included in the invertebrate or "reef" aquarium, and all are excellent choices for smaller marine tanks. Most of the members of these remaining fish families remain under four inches in size.

• HAWKFISHES

The hawkfish family includes some larger species, as well as several that are highly desirable for small tanks. Hawkfishes characteristically perch atop a rock or other prominence, observing the passing scene, darting out now and then to snatch food, such as shrimps or worms, from the water column. Hawkfishes should not be kept with small shrimps, but will not bother most other species of fishes or invertebrates. Hawkfishes are intolerant of each other, so keep only one per tank.

Flame Hawkfish -- *Neocirrhites armatus* is solid red, with a black stripe down the middle of the back, and a black ring around each eye. As this species comes from deep water, it is usually somewhat more expensive than other hawkfishes, but its droll appearance, peaceful disposition and hardiness make the Flame Hawk an excellent choice for the marine tank.

• BASSLETS

Basslets, also called fairy basslets, grammas, *Pseudochromis* , or dottybacks, are beautiful fishes, easy to keep, and easy to feed. Atlantic basslets are called fairy basslets or grammas, and Indo-Pacific basslets are called dottybacks, or *Pseudochromis*. Grammas can usually be kept together successfuly in groups, providing they have ample hiding places, however, do not attempt to keep Indo-Pacific basslets together, as they will fight.

Royal Gramma -- *Gramma loreto* is purple on the anterior half of the body, and bright yellow on the posterior half; there is a black dot on the dorsal fin. This hardy, inexpensive, and undemanding species is generally found in groups under ledges in fairly deep waters in the Atlantic and Caribbean regions. Grammas have spawned in hobbyist tanks. An equally good choice from the Indo-Pacific is the Strawberry Dottyback, *Pseudochromis porphyreus*. This charming little fish is solid royal purple in color, and needs only a suitable hiding place and regular feeding in order to thrive.

• JAWFISHES

The jawfishes are related to the basslets. Only one species is commonly and widely available, the Yellowheaded Jawfish, *Opisthognathus aurifrons*, from the Atlantic. It is pale in color with a bright yellow head. Jawfishes live in large colonies. Each individual constructs a vertical burrow into which it retreats at the slightest threat of danger. Each fish hovers just above the burrow, snatching small organisms from the water column. The Yellowheaded Jawfish is an ideal choice for a species tank.

• BLENNIES

Blennies can be subdivided into two groups:

a. Combtooth or Eyelash Blennies are vegetarians that spend most of their time on the bottom, peering out from a hole or crevice in the rocks, or perhaps living in an empty snail shell. They may be recognized by the cirri, or "eyelashes" on the head.

Bicolor Blenny -- *Escenius bicolor* from the Indo-Pacific is dark blue-black on the anterior portion of the body, and orange on the posterior portion. It feeds avidly on filamentous and encrusting growths of algae, and will also take other small foods.

b. Fanged Blennies are carnivorous, spending most of their time hovering in open water, and feeding on plankton. They are generally more colorful than the combtooth blennies. The name refers to the fact that these species possess poisonous fangs that are used in defense. If a predator grabs one of these fishes, its mouth will be bitten painfully, and the predator usually spits out the blenny unharmed. These well-armed fishes are peaceful toward their tankmates, however.

Canary Blenny -- *Meiacanthus atrodorsalis* is solid yellow, with a beautiful lyre-shaped tail, and comes only from the island of Fiji, in the South Pacific.

• DRAGONETS

This rather extensive family includes only two species of interest to aquarists, the Mandarinfish, *Synchiropus splendidus,* and the Spotted Mandarin, *Synchiropus picturatus*. Problems with these fishes are generally the result of inadequate feeding, as mandarins feed on very tiny organisms, and do so almost constantly during the day. They should only be placed in a well-established aquarium that has a visible population of small crustaceans and other organisms living in it. Male mandarins can be distinguished from females by the presence of a greatly elongated spine at the forward edge of the dorsal fin. Females have a small, unadorned dorsal fin. You can keep several individuals of both mandarin species together in the same tank, as long as there are not two males of the same species, which will fight bitterly.

• GOBIES

The several families of gobies are collectively by far the largest group of marine fishes, in terms of the number of species. Their lifestyles are too varied to make sweeping generalizations, but most gobies are peaceful, colorful, small fishes that can be kept with a variety of other species. For aquarium purposes, we can subdivide the gobies into three large groups:

a. Torpedo Gobies are elongate, midwater fishes that dart rapidly from place to place in the tank, and snatch their food from the water column. Small, meaty aquarium foods are readily accepted.

Firefish -- *Nemateleotris magnifica* are cream colored, with a striking, red, orange and black tail. Unless you have a mated pair, keep only one firefish per tank, as they may fight with each other.

b. Prawn Gobies are distinguished by their special relationship with certain types of shrimps. In this arrangement, the shrimp, which is blind, digs a burrow that both shrimp and goby occupy. The goby provides a pair of eyes. When the two venture forth from their burrow, the shrimp maintains contact with the goby by means of its antennae. If the goby detects danger, a flick of its tail warns the shrimp that it is time to retreat to the burrow. Keep the goby and the shrimp together in the aquarium, as the goby will not fare well without its partner. A pair, along with various invertebrates, could be kept alone in a ten gallon tank. A commonly available prawn goby is the Bluespotted Yellow Watchman, *Cryptocentrus cinctus*.

    c. All other gobies can be lumped together in a diverse assemblage, about which few generalizations can be made, except to say that they make good community fishes for small tanks, or for reef tanks. One "typical" example is the Neon Goby, *Gobiosoma oceanops*, from the Atlantic. Once collected in the Florida Keys, this species is now available from hatchery-reared stock. With a maximum size of about two inches, the Neon Goby is striped horizontally in black, white and blue. This color pattern identifies it as a "cleaner" that picks parasites and dead tissue from the skin of other fishes. The goby will exhibit this beneficial behavior in the aquarium.

    There are literlly dozens of books that will provide you with additional information about marine aquarium fishes. I have already mentioned Burgess's *Atlas of Marine Aquarium Fishes*. Other good choices are the many regional guides available that cover a specific area of the world, such as Hawaii, or the Caribbean. One new book that is outstanding in its information content is *Marine Aquarist Manual Comprehensive Edition*, by Dr. Paul Loiselle and Hans Baensch, published by Tetra Press. For complete coverage of the smaller species in the families described above, you should consult *Fishes for the Invertebrate Aquarium*, by Helmut Debelius, published by Aquarium Systems. All of these books are widely available by mail, or through aquarium dealers.

Chapter Seven
STARTING RIGHT WITH INVERTEBRATES

Most beginning marine enthusiasts start out with fishes. Many ignore, or even avoid invertebrates, perhaps thinking that such unfamiliar creatures may be very difficult to keep. On the contrary, invertebrates, if one understands their special needs, are in many ways hardier and less demanding than marine fishes. In addition, there are plenty of invertebrate species that make good candidates for small aquariums. With reef tanks the current rage, beginners often get the impression that all invertebrates require complicated, expensive filtration and lighting systems. While it is certainly true that high-tech reef tanks provide ideal aquarium conditions for many invertebrates, such systems are hardly necessary for all invertebrate species. And invertebrates do come in great variety. For example, there are about 20,000 species of fishes in the world, marine and freshwater. There are over a million species of invertebrates, and we are still counting. Granted, most of these are insects, but there are probably more species of marine arthropods, alone, than the combined total of all vertebrate species. With over 600 million years of evolutionary history behind them, the invertebrates are a diverse assemblage, indeed.

Biologists sort the bewildering array of invertebrate forms into some 30 large groups, called *phyla* (singular *phylum*). Of these, representatives of six are of interest to aquarists. Of the remaining phyla, several are well represented on aquarium specimens of live rock, for example, but otherwise are seldom seen or discussed by aquarium hobbyists. The six major phyla of interest to aquarists are sponges (Phylum *Porifera*); sea anemones and their relatives (Phylum *Coelenterata*); certain worms (Phylum *Annelida*); mollusks (Phylum *Mollusca*); shrimps and their relatives (Phylum *Arthropoda*); and starfish and their relatives (Phylum *Echinodermata*). An understanding of the varied lifestyles of invertebrates is essential to their successful husbandry in the aquarium. Aquarists, however, need not concern themselves with the details of the natural history of every species. Rather, learning to recognize the broad categories of feeding habits and behavior, which often cut across lines of biological classification, is of more utility to the aquarium keeper. Like fishes, marine invertebrates require that water conditions in the tank be maintained correctly.

Consult the table at the end of Chapter Four for the correct values for your aquarium's water. If you maintain these parameters in your tank with little deviation from day to day, you will be able to keep any invertebrates that you wish, provided you understand their special needs. For the beginner with an interest in invertebrates, the first major distinction that should be recognized is between invertebrates with a requirement for bright light, and those that do not require special tank lighting.

• PHOTOSYNTHETIC INVERTEBRATES

Light-requiring invertebrates need a light intensity of *at least* 10,000 lumens per square meter (lux) in order to survive and grow. Without getting into a long discussion of the merits of various lighting methods, suffice it to say that this level of lighting can be achieved only with fixtures that allow for multiple fluorescent lamps, or by metal halide lighting systems. Give careful consideration, therefore, to the lighting system, if you intend to keep any of the light-requiring species discussed below. (See the box at the end of theis chapter for more lighting information.)

The majority of light-requiring invertebrates are in Phylum *Coelenterata* , the coelenterates (pronounced so-LEN-ter ates). This group includes anemones, corals, soft corals, gorgonians, sea mats, mushroom corals, and all other types of polyp animals. There are a few exceptions, such as the orange polyp coral, *Tubastrea*, that live in darkness, but, in the main, tropical coelenterates all need bright light to survive more than a few weeks. This is because these organisms harbor symbiotic algae, *zooxanthellae*, in their tissues. The algae are absolutely required for the health of the colenterate, and the algae, in turn, require light to carry out photosynthesis. In a properly illuminated aquarium, coelenterates with zooxanthellae need no feeding at all, deriving all of their nourishment from their symbionts. (Exceptional coleenterates, like *Tubastrea*, mentioned above, do need to be fed regularly, however. These coelenterates seem in general to be more demanding aquarium inhabitants than the light-requiring species.)

Apart from coelenterates, the only other light-requiring invertebrates that you are likely to encounter are the giant clams. There are seven species, of which five are available to aquarists from a hatchery in the South Pacific. The most commonly seen of these is *Tridacna derasa*. The zooxanthellae of *Tridacna* impart beautiful colors and patterns to the animal, and no doubt account for the popularity of the giant clams as aquarium subjects. No two clams are exactly alike in color and pattern. Giant clams subsist entirely on the photosynthesis performed by their zooxanthellae, absorbing only oxygen and inorganic nutrients from the water. They grow large, and can live to be very old.

With regard to invertebrates that have no special lighting requirements, all of those we will mention in the remainder of this discussion, the mode of feeding is probably the most important factor to consider when choosing specimens. Apart from photosynthesis by zooxanthellae, there are many feeding modes among invertebrates. Here are the most common ones, with a few examples that you may see in your local aquarium shop.

• FILTER FEEDING

Known by a variety of other names, "suspension feeding", "particle feeding", etc., filter feeding consists of straining the surrounding water for small, planktonic food organisms. Filter feeding invertebrates have a variety of nets, strainers, and other fishing gear that they use for the purpose. Some are passive, simply extending their capture equipment into the water and waiting for currents to bring food. Others pump water through their bodies, and possess internal organs that do the filtering. Among the latter groups are sponges, and bivalve mollusks such as clams. In the former category are worms such as the feather duster and Christmas tree worms, as well as a few unusual arthropods, for example, anemone crabs.

• HERBIVORY

Herbivorous organisms are those that ingest plant matter as the bulk of their diet. Generally, algae is scraped or nibbled from the surface of rocks and other objects. Sea urchins are all herbivorous grazers, as are many kinds of snails. Herbivorous organisms are among the easiest to care for, as they very often subsist entirely upon algae growth that occurs naturally in the tank.

• OMNIVORY

Omnivores eat both plant and animal matter, and many of the invertebrates that fall into this group are considered "scavengers". Most shrimps, crabs and hermit crabs are omnivorous, as well as some mollusks, such as coweries. Large, omnivorous mollusks should be avoided in an aquarium that features a variety of encrusting invertebrates.

• PREDATION

Only a few aquarium invertebrates are active predators, and most of these are either mollusks or arthropods. Large arthropods, crabs and lobsters especially, cannot be trusted not to prey upon smaller tankmates. Among mollusks, it is important to make sure you can identify the species in question, as this may be an important key to its feeding habits. One mollusk in particular, the octopus, is an active predator that will hunt down and eat any tankmates.

This has been a thumbnail summary of invertebrate requirements and lifestyles. While it is not possible to cover the gamut of invertebrate types in a single chapter such as this, it is relatively easy to select a few specific examples from among the most commonly available and popular invertebrate species.

SPONGES

Brightly colored sponges often appear in shops that stock a variety of invertebrates. Most sponges do well if their few simple requirements are met. Above all, they should never be removed from the water, as air trapped inside the sponge will lead to a slow death from within. Otherwise, protect them from overgrowths of algae or accumulations of debris and sponges are long-lived and undemanding aquarium inhabitants.

COELENTERATES

This group is so diverse that only one representative from each of the major subdivisions can be included here.

Anemones

Most people want an anemone as a host for clownfish. Among the most widely available of the clownfish anemones is the Long Tentacle Anemone, *Macrodactyla doreensis*. This species has a salmon-colored column, with tentacales that range in color from brown to bright purple.   It is a good host for many species of clowns, such as the tomato clown, *Amphiprion frenatus* , and the Maroon Clown, *Premnas biaculeatus*

This anemone likes to bury its column in the sub-strate, and gravel or sand should be provided. Given proper lighting and good water quality, it will thrive easily. Never buy an anemone that shows the slightest outward sign of injury, such a tear or puncture, as this may lead to a fatal bacterial infection. Many coelenterates, including anemones, are capable of affecting their relatives in a negative way, even from some distance away. For this reason, clownfish host anemones, in particular, should not be housed in a tank that also contains other coelenterates, unless one knows from experience that the anemone will not be "nettled" by the other species. If nettling does occur, the anemone is usually the loser. Anemones that wander all over the tank (except in the first day or two after they are introduced) are seeking conditions that are more to their liking. A wandering anemone is always an unhappy anemone, and will die in a matter of weeks if its needs are not promptly satisfied.

Since anemones in general, and clownfish host anemones in particular, are rather touchy aquarium subjects, and since they reproduce slowly in nature and live to be very old, many authorities now advise only experienced aquarists to attempt to keep an anemone. I concur with this view. Far too many of these beautiful, interesting invertebrates die as a result of poor handling after they are taken from the sea. This is a needless waste. The Florida Pink-Tipped Anemone, *Condylactis passiflora* , is a suitable anemone for the beginner, and can form the centerpiece of a small invertebrate tank. This species is common in sea grass beds in the Florida Keys, and can be kept with other animals found in this habitat. Consult *Field Guide to the Coral Reefs of Florida and the Bahamas* by Dr. Eugene Kaplan for details about this habitat and the species it contains.

Corals

True corals, those that produce a skeleton of calcium carbonate, should not be attempted by the beginning aquarist. However, after you have gained experience and are ready for a true reef tank with corals, you might consider Elegance Coral, *Catalaphyllia jardineri*, as a first specimen. This species is hardy, grows well in the aquarium (can double in size in six months), and comes in various attractive shades of green, greenish brown, and occassionally, tinges of pink. It tends to be among the more expensive corals, but is well worth the price paid.

Soft corals

Soft corals do not produce a hard, rigid skeleton. Leather Mushroom Soft Coral, *Sarcophyton trocheliophorum*, is a commonly seen species. The fleshy body is shaped like a large toadstool, and is usually light tan or brown in color. Whitish or yellowish polyps dot the upper surface. It requires very bright light, and a high, stable pH, and is generally easy to keep, with specimens regularly producing offspring in the tank. From time to time, this and many other soft coral species may appear shrunken and unhappy. This behavior is apparently normal and should not be cause for alarm unless it persists for over a week. In that case, a large water change may be in order.

Gorgonians

These are soft corals in which the skeleton is rigid, but is not made of calcium carbonate. The texture of the skeleton in gorgonians is similar to that of fingernails or horn, rigid, but flexible. These colonial coelenterates are often very colorful. All gorgonians require good water movement, and abundant food, and are not for beginners.

Sea mats

If you see what appears to be a group of little anemones all connected together at the base, you may be looking at a sea mat. These are hardy, colonial coelenterates that need only bright light to do well. I have seen the Green Sea Mat, *Zoanthus sociatus*, exposed at low tide and baking in the tropical sun. No special care is needed, apart from light and good water quality.

False or Mushroom corals

These coelenterates are sometimes called "false" corals. Most are disk-like polyps about the size of a half dollar, and are usually sold as a cluster of individuals attached to a rock. They are hardy, undemanding species that do not require as much light as their cousins. There are many species of mushroom corals, in the genera *Actinodiscus*, *Rhodactis*, *Amplexidiscus*, *Discosoma*, *Paradiscosoma*, and *Ricordea*. The last one mentioned, which comes from Florida, was once quite popular and commonplace. It is far less frequently seen now, owing to collecting restrictions.

ANNELIDS

Only a few of the thousands of species of segmented marine worms are imported for the aquarium trade. Without exception, these are filter feeders. The primary attraction is the fan-like crown of tentacles, which are employed in both feeding and respiration. In the Giant Hawaiian Feather Duster Worm, *Sabellastarte sanctijosephi*, the appearance of the crown of tentacles gives the animal its name. This species lives in harbors, on docks and pilings, even embedded in mud, and is very hardy in the aquarium. From time to time, the worm may cast off its crown of tentacles. They will grow back in a few weeks, if tank conditions are good.

MOLLUSKS

Mollusks can cause great confusion, simply because there are so many of them. Bivalves, snails and cephalopods are all available from aquarium dealers. Bivalves are all filter feeders, and are typified by the

Flame Scallop, *Lima scabra*, from Florida and the Caribbean. They seldom last long in the aquarium. Cephalopods, such as the octopus, are all predatory. These creatures make difficult aquarium subjects, and have a naturally short life span of one to three years. Most octopus in the aquarium trade are gravid females that will lay eggs in the tank and guard them assiduously until they hatch. The mother will then promptly die, which is Nature's way, alas, and the offspring will prove themselves fiendishly difficult to rear and are cannibalistic, as well. Beginners should avoid this curious, highly intelligent creature.

With snails, of which there are about 50,000 species, and a lot of suitable aquarium types, make sure you can correctly identify the species in which you are interested, as this information will be crucial to determining feeding preferences. Some snails may be predatory and destroy other tank inhabitants, while other snails may be so fussy about their diet that they will starve for lack of the appropriate, specific food organism they require. I repeat, make sure you know the species you are getting before you add any snail to the aquarium. Snails in the genera *Turbo* and *Astraea* are widely sold for algae control.

ARTHROPODS

Most arthropods are omnivores, and are easy to keep. The Banded Coral Shrimp, *Stenopus hispidus*, for example, will thrive on bits of food missed by the fishes, as will the Scarlet Cleaner Shrimp, *Lysmata grabhami* , or *L. amboiensis.*   Either of these shrimps may be seen in almost any dealer's tanks.   In nature, both these shrimps are cleaners, removing parasites, dead tissue, etc., from fishes. Only the Scarlet Cleaner is prone to exhibit this behavior in the aquarium, however.

ECHINODERMS

This phylum includes starfish, brittle stars, sea urchins and sea cucumbers. Sea cucumbers are filter feeders, urchins are grazing herbivores, brittle stars are omnivorous scavengers. Starfish may be herbivores or predators, and it is important to know the difference, for obvious reasons. Among the commonly seen starfish, the Blue Star, *Linckia laevigata*, is vegetarian, and can safely be housed with other invertebrates. Predatory starfish, like the Bahama Star, *Oreaster reticulata*, will eventually eat anything that is slow-moving enough for the star to catch.

Invertebrates are so varied that books are essential to the invertebrate aquarium enthusiast. Of the many titles on the market, one of the best is *The Manual of Marine Invertebrates*, by Martyn Haywood and Sue Wells, published by Tetra Press. Along with informative text, this book provides excellent color photographs of correctly identified invertebrates that are widely seen in aquarium shops. There are literally dozens of other titles that are useful to the marine hobbyist. These most often deal with the species found in a particular region of the world, or with the biology of a particular phylum of invertebrates. A good introduction to invertebrate biology is the college textbook, *Invertebrate Zoology*, by Dr. Robert Barnes, publishes by the W.B. Saunders Publishing Company. You can find it in college bookstores, or at the library.

With such variety to choose from, invertebrates are gaining in popularity among aquarists. Sooner or later, you will want to try them, too. Just make sure you read up on the species in which you are interested before you buy.

/

Chapter Eight
ANY QUESTIONS?

You know by now that maintaining a successful saltwater aquarium entails three key points. These are:

• **Your tank must be large enough to accommodate the specimens you keep, and it must have a properly conditioned biological filter, as well as some form of chemical filtration. In my opinion, the ideal form of chemical filtration is the protein skimmer.**

• **You must perform regular maintenance and testing, paying special attention to partial water changes, and keep accurate and complete records.**

• **You must learn about the biology of the species you intend to keep, in order to provide them with adequate space, compatible tankmates, and an appropriate, nutritious diet.**

Marine aquarium keeping is as much an art as it is a science. As you gain experience, inevitably, questions arise that are not answered in the literature, at least not directly. Here are some of the questions that hobbyists have most commonly asked me over the past few years, together with the answers.

1. Why are marine fish so expensive compared to freshwater fish?

This is the first question almost every beginning marine hobbyist asks. The answer is simple: most freshwater fish are produced in hatcheries in Florida and the Far East, and can be shipped in huge quantities at very low cost. Marine fish, on the other hand, must be collected from the wild (with the exception of a few species), and require more space in a shipping container if they are to arrive alive. This translates into a higher cost, both for the fish and for air freight. In addition, maintaining many tanks for marine fishes is more costly for the retailer than maintaining the same number of tanks for freshwater species. All of these added costs are reflected in the retail price of the fish.

2. I have had problems with parasites, how can I eliminate them permanently from my tank?

This is a commonplace question that stems from a fundamental misunderstanding of the nature of the two parasites most frequently seen in marine fishes. First, the parasites themselves are ubiquitous, and cannot be "eliminated" from the aquarium. The key to avoiding an infestation is to provide conditions that promote good health in the fish population. In the ocean, the fish's immune system largely protects it from infestations of *Cryptocaryon* (white spot) and *Amlyoodinium*. In the aquarium, maintaining good health in the fishes involves, first and foremost, practicing good aquarium management. When you bring a new specimen home from the dealer, place it in a separate tank for a couple of weeks to observe its behavior. This will prevent any problem that may develop in the new fish from spreading to other, established specimens. In addition, isolating new specimens in a separate tank makes the job of treating them much easier, if a need for treatment does develop.

Should treatment for white spot or coral fish disease become necessary, the only truly effective medication is copper. Use an ionic (not "chelated") copper medication, and use a copper test kit to determine when the correct dosage has been added to the treatment tank. A copper concentration of 0.15 - 0.20 ppm is most effective. Below 0.15 ppm, the treatment will not be effective; above 0.20 ppm, the copper is stressful to the fishes. Copper medications should never be used in a tank containing invertebrates, as most invertebrates are rapidly killed by therapeutic levels of copper. This is another good reason to have a separate treatment tank.

Angelfishes are somewhat more sensitive to copper treatment. Before exposing an infected angelfish to copper, attempt to cure the problem with a medication containing formaldehyde and malachite green, applied according to the manufacturer's directions.

Symptoms of *Cryptocaryon* and *Amyloodinium* include rapid shallow breathing, scratching, hiding, poor appetite, loss of color, and the appearance of small white dots on the fish's body and fins. These parasite problems commonly appear in fishes that have recently been transported from the point of capture, and in tanks that have experienced some sudden departure from good water conditions. In short, when a fish is under stress, it is more likely to succumb to a parasite infestation.

In my experience, more aquarium fishes are killed by *Amyloodinium* than by *Cryptocaryon* . In fact, I think deaths attributed to *Cryptocaryon* have actually been the result of *Amyloodinium,* with the other parasite a secondary invader. I have seen fishes recover from *Cryptocaryon* without treatment. This has not been the case with *Amyloodinium* . Further, it is known that the latter parasite produces a substance, apparently not unlike that involved in "red tides", that is toxic to fishes. This is in addition to the *Amyloodinium* organism's penchant for feeding upon and destroying the fish's gills, causing death by oxygen starvation if left untreated.

Beginners may not be able to diagnose *Amyloodinium* until it is too late to save the infected fish, because by the time external symptoms appear, the damage to the gills has already been done. My advice to beginners is simple: if any fish in the tank appears to be breathing at a more rapid rate than the others, or more rapidly than you are accustomed to seeing as a "normal" breathing rate, treat the entire fish population promptly with copper. The breathing rate in fishes is somewhat influenced by temperature, so all the fishes in the same tank should be breathing at the same rate, under normal circumstances. Chasing a fish with a net, for example, will increase its breathing rate, but in this case, the rate returns to normal after a few minutes. This is analogous to what happens to you if you are walking down the street and have to break into a run suddenly to catch the bus. For several minutes after you finally board the bus, your breathing rate will be rapid , and will return to normal as your body adjusts itself. When a fish's gills are damaged by a parasite infestation, the fish breathes more rapidly to compensate, and normal breathing does not resume until the infestation is alleviated.

3. How can I get rid of all this algae?

It is worthwhile to point out that many species of marine life feed on algae. Tangs, angelfishes, some blennies, and many kinds of snails are in this category. These species will benefit from being able to graze on algae growth in the tank. Algae becomes a "problem" when it interferes with the aesthetic appeal of the tank, or when rampant growth threatens to smother delicate organisms such as sessile invertebrates.

There is no simple solution to the problem of controlling excess algae growth, because a variety of factors are involved. Of primary importance in the closed system of a marine aquarium is the accumulation of excessive levels of nutrient ions in the tank. Nitrate, phosphate, carbon dioxide and dissolved organic matter all play a role. These substances are in relatively short supply in the natural environment of the coral reef. In the aquarium, however, they can rapidly accumulate, providing "fertilizer" for explosive growths of filamentous, encrusting, and free floating algae species.

Removal of dissolved organic matter by means of a protein skimmer is one of the simplest techniques of algae control, although this approach alone will not work if attention is not paid to the other nutrients, as well. Protein skimmers also tend to lower the concentration of carbon dioxide in the water, as a result of vigorous aeration that takes place in the skimmer column. Step one, then, in any plan to prevent algae from taking over your tank, is to install a protein skimmer, and to keep it properly maintained.

Limiting the concentration of nitrates and phosphates is a bit more complicated. Nitrate, for example, constantly accumulates in the aquarium as the end product of biological filtration. Most of the nitrogen present in foods added to the tank winds up as nitrate. Regular partial water changes are one means of controlling nitrate. The amount and frequency of water changes will depend on the particular circumstances of each individual aquarium. Thus, one should perform a nitrate test weekly, and change water when the concentration of nitrate ion rises above 10 parts per million (ppm). As a general rule, more frequent water changes are required for tanks that are densely populated with fish, and less frequent changes are required for tanks that are largely populated with invertebrates.

Phosphate limitation is a more effective means of algae control than is nitrate limitation, but presents a somewhat more complicated problem from a practical point of view.   Phosphate is ubiquitous in nature, and finds its way into the aquarium from a variety of sources. These include all foods, some salt mixes and tank additives, and especially tap water. In every case that I have had the opportunity to investigate, a tank overgrown with algae also contains a high concentration of phosphate. Keeping your aquarium scrupulously clean, and particularly the removal of accumulated detritus on a regular basis, will help to eliminate phosphates. If your salt mix contains phosphates, switch to a brand that does not. You can evaluate your current brand easily by performing a phosphate test on a freshly mixed batch of water. You should perform a phosphate test on a sample of your tap water, also. If the tap water contains phosphates, you will have to decide if your algae problem is sufficiently severe to warrant purifying the tap water before use, by means of reverse osmosis, deionization, or some other means. If your water requirements are small, you can purchase distilled water at the grocery store.

Filter media are available that will remove nitrates and phosphates. Such media can be used to limit the concentration of these compounds, but remember that they are of little value for a tank that has high levels of nutrients to begin with. After you have eliminated nitrate and phosphate by the methods outlined above, you can use ion-removers to help keep these problem ions under control, if necessary.

One type of algae growth may be particularly troublesome in newly established tanks. Golden brown films that spread across the glass, substrate and decorations are growths of diatoms. Diatoms require, in addition to the other nutrients mentioned above, a compound called silica that is most often found in tap water. Fortunately, diatom growth is often replaced by other types of algae as the tank matures. If your tank develops an unremitting problem with this type of algae, the only satisfactory solution is to use purified water, not tap water, for making synthetic seawater.

Lighting also plays a role in algae growth. For example, in tanks that formerly grew little algae, the appearance of a bloom of diatoms, red slime algae, or blue-green slime algae is often indicative of the need to change fluorescent lamps. As lamps age, their intensity diminishes and their spectral output changes, and this may trigger a growth of undesirable algae where none was previously present. The relationship between light and marine life is complicated and poorly understood, however. For more information about the complex nature of algae growth in the aquarium, consult other references in books and hobbyist magazines. Much is being written about this perennial problem.

4. What are those little bugs crawling on the glass?

After an aquarium has been established for a while, tiny crustaceans and worms sometimes appear. These are probably introduced into the tank along with fish and invertebrate specimens, and feed on detritus and algae. The commonly observed species are capable of reproduction in the tank, and sometimes multiply to high population densities. Several organisms are in this category.

Amphipods are shrimplike crustaceans about a quarter of an inch in length. Copepods, another crustacean, are much smaller, and may appear as white specks moving around on the glass and rocks. Flatworms are about an eighth of an inch long, with a rounded head end and forked tail in the most commonly seen species. They are translucent, and are usually seen gliding on the glass. Nematodes are short, white, threadlike worms usually less than a quarter inch in length. All of these are harmless scavengers, but their presence in great abundance indicates that excessive detritus is accumulating in the tank, or that uneaten food or a dead animal is decomposing in the tank unnoticed. Cleaning the tank will lower the numbers of these organisms.

While not in the "little bug" category, bristleworms can also reproduce in the aquarium, and these may indeed pose a problem. Bristleworms are usually pinkish orange in color, with rows of white bristles running along the sides of their bodies. They may grow to about three inches in length, and can infest the substrate over an undergravel filter in enormous numbers. The bristles can irritate your skin, if they come into contact, and the worms have been known to feed on sessile invertebrates, causing extensive damage. They may be eliminated, if you are patient, by baiting with a piece of shrimp or fish fillet wrapped in nylon mesh (such as a piece of pantyhose). Tie a string to the bait bundle and lower it into the tank after the lights are out. Wait a half hour or so, and lift out the bundle with worms clinging to it. Swish them off in a bucket of freshwater, and return the bait to the tank to catch another batch. Keep this up every evening until the population is under control. Also keep the detritus vacuumed out of the tank. Several organisms, including fishes in the genus *Pseudochromis* and the Arrow Crab (*Stenorhynchus seticornis*) will greatly assist in keeping these worms under control. Arrow crabs may feed on other, desirable worms species, however, so use caution.

5. *What kind of lighting do I need to use?*

If your aquarium contains no invertebrates or plants that require intense, wide spectrum illumination, almost any fluorescent lighting system will suffice. If, on the other hand, you plan to stock species that require light, such as anemones, you must give the lighting system more thought. In this short space, I cannot discuss all of the factors that must be taken into account in the design of a lighting system for photosynthetic inverte-

brates.   Suffice it to say that many lighting systems
will work, and you should carefully research the available information before choosing the lighting for your
particular application.

6. Which tank additives should I use?

I'm not a big fan of tank additives, especially those
that contain "vitamins", "growth factors", or other organic components. Certain inorganic additives may
prove useful, however. For fish-only tanks, chemical
powders that buffer the pH and increase alkalinity may
be used, if your test results indicate that such action is
necessary. Alternatively, you can just do partial water
changes more frequently.

For tanks with invertebrates, and particularly for
reef tanks, certain additives may be required to maintain proper levels of some specific ions that these organisms remove from the water. Most commonly, a
calcium supplement is needed to maintain the calcium
concentration of the tank at about 400 ppm. Use should
be predicated upon regular testing of the water for calcium. Calcium is also lost from the water by chemical
precipitation.

Corals and other organisms that manufacture a
calcium carbonate skeleton or shell need strontium as
well as calcium. Many reef hobbyists have reported
excellent growth and development of these invertebrates
when a strontium supplement is used in addition to calcium. Iodine is required by soft corals, crustaceans,

and other invertebrates, and can be added in small amounts on a regular basis. You cannot test for either strontium or iodine, so you must depend upon the recommendations of the supplement manufacturer for an appropriate dosing schedule.

Do not depend on mixtures of "trace elements" to supply the compounds just mentioned in appropriate amounts, and note that you need none of these in a fish only tank. Furthermore, you may not need additives in an invertebrate tank, either. I suggest that you monitor and maintain the correct calcium concentration, along with the other tank parameters I have previously discussed, using calcium supplements, and pH and alkalinity adjusters *only* , based upon the results you obtain with test kits. After you have established a routine of this kind of water quality maintenance, choose a single additive preparation, a strontium supplement, for example, and use the preparation according to its label directions for two months. At the end of that time, evaluate the appearance and health of the specimens in the tank, and make a decision as to whether this additive has proven its usefulness in your particular situation. It may be extremely helpful to take a photograph of the tank before you begin this evaluation process, and again at intervals to help you assess the condition of the organisms in the tank.

If you think your fish need additional vitamins, add a vitamin supplement to the food, not to the tank water.

7. Which salt mix is the best one?

There is actually no "best" brand of salt mix, and no synthetic mix is as satisfactory as natural seawater. Unfortunately, the majority of aquarists do not have natural seawater available, and must rely on a synthetic mix. I have used various brands over the years, with mostly good results. If you are trying to limit the concentration of phosphates in your tank (see the discussion of algae control, above), select a mix that does not contain phosphates detectable with your test kit. If you are considering switching brands, buy a bag of the new brand and mix up a batch. Allow the mix to sit overnight, preferably with aeration, to permit the salts to completely dissolve and the pH to stabilize. Then test this batch for pH (which should be 8.3.), alkalinity (which should be 3.5 meq/l or more), calcium (should be 400 ppm or more) and phosphate (should be zero). If the mix passes muster, use it.

8. What do I do in case of a power failure?

In a well-maintained marine tank that is not overcrowded, a power outage of a few hours is not usually cause for concern. If the outage extends beyond about four hours, you can take the following precautions to protect your fishes:

• **Cover the tank with a heavy quilt or blanket to retard heat loss.**

• **Aerate the water every half hour by dipping some out with a clean pitcher and pouring it back into the tank from a height of about one foot, to agitate the water and promote gas exchange.**

• **As soon as power is restored, check to make sure all equipment has restarted properly, and plan to do a partial water change the following day.**

• **If the outage has lasted longer than eight hours, test the tank for ammonia, nitrite, pH and alkalinity, and observe the inhabitants carefully for problems that may develop over the next several days. If a week goes by without noticeable trouble, you can rest easy.**

If you live in an area that is subject to frequent power outages of long duration, you might want to consider a battery operated air pump as a back up, or, if your fish collection is a valuable one, an emergency generator.

9. How do I know if I am feeding my fish properly?

First, learn all you can about the natural diet of the fishes you intend to keep, and try to duplicate this as closely as possible in the aquarium. Second, feed as wide a variety of foods as possible. Third, experiment. Try different brands and types of foods available from your dealer. It is best to buy foods in small quantities that will be used up quickly. Each time you need food, buy one that you have not used recently. Also experiment with fresh seafoods and greens from the grocery store. Providing a nutritious, varied diet is one of the easiest and least costly aspects of maintaining a marine tank.   Feed your fish twice daily if they are in a fish-only system, or two or three times a week if they are in a reef tank with abundant live rock, microinvertebrates, and algae., Feed only what is completely consumed within a few minutes. Be sure to remove uneaten food promptly from the tank.

10. Can you suggest some good books on marine aquariums?

Here are some references that should be on every marine aquarist's library shelf, in my view:

Allen, Gerald, and Daphne Fautin. *Field Guide to the Anemonefishes and Their Host Anemones* , Western Australian Museum Press, Perth, WA, Australia. 160 pp.

Debelius, Helmut. *Fishes for the Invertebrate Aquarium* , Aquarium Systems, Mentor, OH. 160 pp.

Haywood, Martyn and Sue Wells. *Manual of Marine Invertebrates*, Tetra Press, Morris Plains, NJ. 208 pp.

Mills, Dick. *Encyclopedia of the Marine Aquarium*, Tetra Press, Morris Plains, NJ. 208 pp.

Moe, Martin. *The Marine Aquarium Handbook, Beginner to Breeder*, Green Turtle Publications, Plantation, FL. 176 pp.

Moe, Martin. *The Marine Aquarium Reference, Systems and Invertebrates,* Green Turtle Publications, Plantation, FL. 510 pp.

Thiel, Albert. *The Marine Fish and Invert Reef Aquarium*, Aardvark Press, Mesilla Park, NM. 320 pp.

Tullock, John. *The Reef Tank Owner's Manual* , Aardvark Press, Mesilla Park, NM. 272 pp.

There are also many books that cover the fishes and/or invertebrates of specific regions of the world's oceans. Choose from among these according to your interests. Some titles that I have found useful are:

Kaplan, Dr. Eugene. *A Field Guide to Coral Reefs of Florida and the Bahamas*, Houghton-Miflin, New York. 289 pp.

Myers, Robert F. *Micronesian Reef Fishes* , Coral Graphics, Guam. 298 pp.

Chapter Nine
READY FOR A REEF TANK

By now, I hope that your marine tank is up and running, and looking great. If you have been following the advice I have presented, it should be. After all of those visits to the aquarium store, you probably have developed an interest in marine invertebrates, and you are perhaps thinking of setting up a reef tank. This chapter is designed to help you decide if you really want a reef tank, and, if so, to offer some brief guidelines as to how to proceed.

I wrote an entire book on reef tanks, and there are several other great books on the subject currently available. Therefore, it should be obvious that I cannot cover all the possibilities in the few words that follow. What I hope to do is to dispel some of the myths surrounding reef tanks, in the hope that more people will cultivate an interest in the fascinating world of marine invertebrates.

Most hobbyists have come to associate the words "reef tank" with visions of huge, expensive and complicated systems that are beyond the ken of the average person. Nothing could be further from the truth. If attention is paid to establishing a proper setup, and to monitoring water quality on a regular basis, anyone can have a successful, beautiful reef tank. Here is how to do it:

Myth #1: "Reef tanks must be large to be successful."

Baloney! One of the prettiest reef tanks I have seen holds 1 and 1/2 gallons of water. Four of my employees have 10 gallon reef tanks, and we have one sitting on our sales counter, as well. All of these small tanks are thriving, and best of all, the cost was minimal.

Myth #2: "A successful reef tank requires a trickle filter, along with lots of automated equipment."

More baloney. Only two pieces of equipment (other than the tank itself) are essential -- a protein skimmer, and a lighting system of sufficient intensity. For small tanks, these requirements are easily met.

If the foregoing has sufficiently caught your interest, read further for a step-by-step "recipe" for establishing your own miniature reef.

First, decide on how large your tank will be. Any size will do, but a 20 gallon tank may prove most convenient, as lighting equipment is readily available for a 24 inch long tank. (Of course, you can begin with a really large tank, if your desires and budget permit, but for the remainder of our discussion, we will assume that the tank is 20 gallons.) Purchase a light fixture that will accommodate two 20-watt fluorescent lamps, and in this fixture install two lamps of the highest possible intensity. Also purchase a protein skimmer. This will become the heart of the aquarium's filtration system, and it is important to select one that is appropriate for the tank. You can use a columnar skimmer designed for installation inside the tank, but I like external skimmers, to avoid having a piece of equipment taking up space in the tank and detracting from its natural appearance.

While you are shopping for aquarium equipment, you may as well purchase the test equipment you will need. This includes a thermometer (the digital, stick-on types work well), a hydrometer, and test kits for ammonia, nitrite, nitrate, pH, alkalinity, calcium, and phosphate.

Before you put all of this together, however, give some thought to the water you will be using. Your tap water may not be satisfactory for the demands of reef tank organisms. Thus, you must decide if you will purify your tap water before use, or if you will simply purchase distilled water. For a small system with relatively low needs for purified water, the latter approach may prove the best. If you opt to purify tap water yourself, check out the various reverse osmosis units that are available. By whatever means, however, insure that the fresh water you start with is low in phosphates and other pollutants that will eventually cause problems for your reef system. By the same token, use a high quality salt mix. Remember that the quality of life for your minireef denizens is a direct function of the quality of the water in the aquarium.

Locate your tank in a suitable spot, install the equipment, fill it with properly prepared synthetic seawater, and turn everything on. Make sure that the equipment is functioning properly, and wait 24 hours before going to the next step. If the temperature remains too high after the tank has stabilized and the lights have been on for 12 hours, you will need to locate the tank in a different, cooler spot, or start thinking about a chiller to keep the tank at 75°F. A stable, cool temperature is essential for long-term success with many invertebrates.

The next step is a crucial one. You will add to the tank a sufficient amount of cured live rock. "Cured live rock" is simply carbonate rock taken from the ocean with attached and encrusting organisms intact. After curing, few large organisms will be apparent on the rock's surface, although it will be nicely encrusted with coralline macroalgae in shades of purple and mauve, and may have small invertebrates or green macroalgae colonies present as well. After the rock has been in your aquarium for a while, you may be surprised at the diversity of organisms that appear, as if by magic, but this will take several months. The nature and quality of this material will, more than any other single factor, determine the success of your miniature reef. This has been repeatedly stated by many other authors than myself, and bears repeating yet again. *Do not scrimp on the live rock*. You will need between 20 and 40 pounds of this material to fill the 20 gallon tank in this example, enough to build a loosely constructed ridge extending the length of the tank and roughly three-fourths the height. Cured live rock is far superior to uncured material. The latter may look pretty and interesting to begin with, but will be covered with rotting organisms within about a week. It will generate not only huge quantities of pollutants but also a foul odor as it "cures" in the confines of your system. It is therefore worth the extra expense to obtain cured rock in the first place.

It is not necessary to add all of the live rock at once, provided that you use properly cured material. Do not, however, add other organisms to the tank until all of the live rock is in place. New reef tanks experience what I call a "period of instability" lasting from four to eight weeks after the live rock is added. During this time, the tank will grow various types of algae, often in great abundance. Do not panic at this point, although the tank may look pretty bad. Keep all equipment in operation, and perform routine testing and maintenance as if the tank were filled with corals and anemones. Pay special attention at maintaining the calcium concentration of the tank at 400 ppm, and keep the pH up between 8.3 and 8.5. Before your patience is completely exhausted (I hope), you will awake one morning to discover a tiny new colony of purple coralline macroalgae growing on the glass or elsewhere, where none was apparent before. Rejoice! This is a sure sign that the period of instability is almost over, and the coralline algae will begin to proliferate while other, less desirable algae species begin to decline.

During the period of instability, only hardy organisms should be added to the reef tank. These include herbivorous snails (*Astraea* and *Turbo*), brittlestars, shrimps, fanworms, and fish. Consider the Scarlet Cleaner shrimp, *Lysmata amboiensis* , or the Fire Shrimp, *Lysmata debelius*. If you wish to include a fish or two in this small set-up, good choices would include a dwarf angel (various *Centropyge* species), or Firefish (*Nemateleotris magnifica*), or perhaps a Blue Damsel (*Chrysiptera cyanea*). Remember to keep the fish population small. Select only one or two of the species mentioned above. Feed the fish a small amount two or three times a week, making sure they receive a varied diet.

Once the period of instability has passed, you can add a variety of other organisms to the aquarium. Good choices for the beginning reef enthusiast include the following:

• **Mushroom Polyps, including the many species of *Actinodiscus*, *Discosoma*, or *Rhodactis* generally sold as a colony of several disk-like polyps on a rock;**

• **Zoanthids, also called Sea Mats, various species including the bright yellow *Parazoanthus axinellae*;**

• **Soft corals, including the Leather Corals *Sarcophyton*, *Lobophytum*, and *Sinularia*, and the extremely hardy Green Star Polyp soft coral, *Clavularia viridis*.**

All of these species should be readily available, and all are easy to keep. Among the true, or stony, corals, consider Closed Brain Coral (*Trachyphyllia geoffreyi*), Bubble Coral (*Plerogyra flexuosa*), Elegance Coral (*Catalaphyllia jardineri*), and any of the *Euphyllia* species. The latter genus includes Hammer Coral (*E. ancora*), Frogspawn Coral (*E. divisa*) and Torch Coral (*E. glabrescens*).

Finally, consider adding a Giant Clam. Several species are now available as hatchery-produced specimens. These include *Tridacna derasa*, *T. crocea*, *T. maxima*, and *T. gigas*. All have beautifully colored soft tissues that are filled with symbiotic algae. With proper lighting, giant clams are easy to keep.

In placing specimens in the tank, bear in mind that they can damage each other if physical contact is made. Thus, allow room between the various specimens so that this "nettling" does not occur.

Maintenance

Routine maintenance on your reef tank involves changing one or two gallons of water every week, and testing the tank weekly. Monitor the calcium concentration of the tank with a calcium test kit and use limewater or another calcium supplement to maintain the calcium concentration at 400 ppm. Other than food for the fish (if you choose to include a few small fish in the set-up) do not put organic additives (such as vitamins, enzyme products, "growth factors", etc.) into the tank. Excessive use of organic additives will almost surely lead to an algae bloom. The two most important chemical "enemies" of your microreef system are phosphates and nitrates. Buy good test kits for each of these compounds, and test weekly. If phosphate is above 0.1 ppm, or nitrate climbs above 10 ppm, do a partial water change.

Keep the pH of the tank at least 8.3, but do not allow this parameter to exceed 8.6. You may need to add a buffering preparation to achieve this, although probably not if you use limewater for calcium supplementation. Limewater is a saturated solution of calcium hydroxide (hydrated lime) and is prepared by adding about 2 grams (a rounded teaspoon of calcium oxide (slaked lime, pickling lime) to one gallon of purified water. Use only the clear liquid. There will be some undissolved lime at the bottom of the container. This can be used to make another batch of limewater, if you wish. Caution! Do not get lime or limewater in your eyes or on mucouse membranes, and keep both the dry powder and the prepared limewater out of children's reach. About one ounce of limewater per fifty gallons of aquarium water is a typical rate of addition per day, but you will need to determine the proper amount for your tank by means of a calcium test.

In summary, the key points for setting up a twenty gallon reef tank are:

• Place about one pound per gallon of high quality, cured Pacific islands live rock in the tank.

- Use at least two 20 watt fluorescent lamps.
- Add only enough sand to create a thin layer on the bottom of the tank, or use no substrate material at all.
- The filter system must incorporate a protein skimmer.
- Test water routinely, and perform small partial water changes once a week.
- Maintain calcium at 400 ppm.
- Clean detritus from the filter every week.

A SPECIAL TIP

You can make a protein skimmer for a small marine tank by installing a small columnar skimmer in the box of an outside power filter. Simply run airline tubing from a pump to the skimmer airstone. Turn on the outside power filter and allow the box to fill with water. Turn on the air to the skimmer and adjust. Presto! An external skimmer.

Chapter Ten
NEW TRENDS IN AQUARIUM KEEPING

Keeping "reef" aquariums has become one of the main attractions of the marine aquarium hobby.   Nevertheless, hobbyists really must get used to the fact that one cannot really have a coral reef in the living room anymore than one can drive to work in the space shuttle. The best one can hope for is a display of species that are characteristic of a single microhabitat, a specific, tiny portion of the reef.

Creating a microhabitat display of invertebrates is easier than doing the same for most fishes. This is because fishes can move from one microhabitat to another, while invertebrates, by and large, remain fixed in place, and thus occupy a more limited range of microhabitat types. Properly designed microhabitat display aquariums exhibit a variety of marine invertebrates in an approximation of their natural relationships. "Success" in the endeavor is reflected in the degree to which the living elements of the display survive, develop, and especially, reproduce, as they do in the sea. The "trick", of course, is to arrive at an aquarium system design appropriate for the species that will live in the display.

Creating the type of display that has come to be called a "reef tank" is regarded as an exceptional challenge by many aquarists, beginners in particular. The exotic appearance of most invertebrates leads the novice to conclude that such organisms must be very delicate. In fact, most marine invertebrates are remarkably sturdy if their requirements are understood and supplied.

Another reason that some hobbyists may be reluctant to set up a reef tank has a historical basis. The majority of marine species that today are kept in such aquariums were introduced into the trade as a result of the surge in popularity of "wet/dry" or "trickle" filter systems. From simple beginnings rooted in the technology of municipal wastewater treatment systems, "reef tank" filter systems evolved into complex, expensive collections of apparatus. Many hobbyists found such systems to be too complicated, too expensive, or both.

Today, there are three major new trends that are shaping the way hobbyists approach the "reef tank". The first of these trends I call the "less technology, more biology" trend. Experienced hobbyists approach the husbandry of marine life in terms of the ecological needs of the species of interest, rather than in terms of the availability of technology. As Dr. Stephen Spotte, in his excellent book *Captive Seawater Fishes*, has written, "...I believe strongly that curatorial practices should be based on understanding the biological requirements of captive fishes, not on the application of technology."

Of course, technology cannot be dispensed with entirely, but we must begin the aquarium design by understanding the needs of the species we intend to keep. For example, recognition that most tropical coelenterates require intense, wide spectrum lighting has made a tremendous difference in our ability to keep these species successfully.

One of my favorite analogies is the comparison between a tank full of marine invertebrates and a flower box or garden bed full of terrestrial plants. I am an avid gardener, and I read as many books and magazines about gardening as I do about aquariums. When I open the pages of *Horticulture* or *National Gardening* I am not likely to see articles about the latest advances in design of roto-tiller tines. Rather, I find articles about plants, and these articles always relate to the needs of the plants, not the needs of the gardener. We need more of this kind of thinking in the aquarium hobby.

Marine aquariums based on an understanding of the ecology of marine organisms are easy to maintain, and are likely to provide what a species needs to complete its life cycle. They are "successful" in the sense that success was defined above. When I was setting up tanks in the early 80's to keep specimens of invertebrates and macroalgae, I was simply trying to provide a proper environment for specimens I had brought back from the Florida Keys. I looked upon these aquariums as miniature ecosystems, and I made every effort to duplicate, as closely as possible, the environments that I had observed while snorkeling. I had never heard of actinic lamps or metal halide lighting. Similarly, I knew nothing of limewater, calcium supplements, or ozone. I had heard of protein skimmers, but my local dealer thought they were useless, and I therefore had never seen one.

My methods were imperfect, but one thing that I was doing right was installing multiple fluorescent lamps over the tanks. I tried to balance the spectrum by combining different lamp types, with good success. Another important part of my methods was the use of chunks of rock, with encrusting organisms still attached -- what we now call "live rock". My anemones (*Bartholomea annulata)* grew and thrived. Seaweeds required almost constant pruning. In fact, I had done a very good job of recreating a shallow water habitat. I am sure anyone would agree I had a version of what we now call a "reef tank."

That was many years ago. At that time virtually all marine aquarium hobbyists were keeping what I now call "fish display" tanks. Fish display tanks are still chosen by the majority. (I define a "fish display" as an aquarium with a large fish population and artificial or dead decorations. Fish displays often feature large, spectacular species.)

Today, an ecologically sound aquarium in which are exhibited as many elements as possible of a specific, natural marine environment is the goal. The common features of ecologically sound microhabitat displays are:

• **ample quantities of good quality live rock;**

• **high intensity, broad spectrum lighting;**

• **filtration that focuses on removal of organic wastes rather than mineralization of them;**

• **husbandry that limits the concentrations of certain inorganic ions (nitrate, phosphate), and at the same time insures a constant supply of other inorganic ions (calcium, strontium, iodine, iron) in concentrations that match or exceed those found in the ocean;**

• **replication of the physical characteristics of the microhabitat, in terms of temperature, substrate type, currents, diel cycles, etc.;**

• **attention to the community relationships of the species housed together in the same aquarium.**

To carry on with the gardening analogy, I would rather use my roto-tiller than use a shovel to dig a new vegetable bed. Aquarists will benefit most from technology that permits better measurements of the physical and chemical parameters of the aquarium environment. Electronic meters have already begun to supplant color-change test kits for the measurement of pH, for example. Such instruments are faster, more accurate and easier to read. Good information about conditions in the aquarium is obviously fundamental to successful management of water quality.

The second trend developing within the marine aquarium hobby is a much broader understanding of marine science. Hobbyists with little formal scientific training demonstrate familiarity with scientific principles as they apply to aquarium keeping. This has happened because the chemical, physical and biological relationships among species and their environment are most easily expressed in the terminology of chemistry, physics and biology. What is an aquarium if not a concrete demonstration of the nature of these relationships? The language of science lends precision to our discussions, and helps make sense of the often bewildering diversity of marine life and marine habitats. A greater appreciation of scientific principles will reward hobbyists with reproducibility of results from one aquarium to another.

Of course, we must not ignore the importance of creativity, aesthetics, and wisdom in husbandry practice. Like a garden, an aquarium is an extension into time as well as space. Like the gardener, the aquarist derives pleasure from seeing his or her creation grow and evolve. At the beginning, the aquarist creates a mental image of how the aquarium will look in the future. The degree to which the aquarium actually coincides with this image is the basis of the aquarist's satisfaction with the project.

Some aquarists achieve the desired result with comparative ease. Gardeners call this "having a green thumb." Something similar exists among aquarists, and has nothing to do with science.

The third trend is perhaps the most important to the future of the marine aquarium hobby. This is the trend toward *environmental awareness* among aquarium hobbyists. The development of techniques for keeping a great variety of marine life in home aquariums has fostered an awareness of the marvelous richness, diversity, and beauty of the marine realm. This awareness has, in turn, increased the desire to see these resources preserved and protected. The modern hobbyist must realize that the most environmentally sound way for our hobby to continue to exist in the future is to produce within the hobby all of the species that we are interested in maintaining in our aquariums.

Today, especially among those hobbyists who work with invertebrates, captive propagation of aquarium species is not only possible, but sometimes unavoidable. On a commercial scale, there are still only a few species under production. Several of the anemonefishes and a few gobies constitute the only commercially available captive reared aquarium fish. Many more species could be produced if economic considerations did not make their culture unfeasible. With invertebrates and macroalgae, however, the situation is different. A dozen species of macroalgae are routinely cultured. Probably a great many more could be, with ease. Giant clams (*Tridacna* sp.) are the most popular invertebrates that are commercially cultured, although queen conchs

(*Strombus gigas*), and a few others, are seen from time to time.

The number of species that might potentially be cultured, however, is remarkable, and runs the gamut, phylogenetically speaking. Certain sponges grow very well in my tanks, along with at least three species of sedentary worms, for example. These organisms grow without any particular attention from me. Among the coelenterates, virtually all mushroom polyps, sea mats and soft corals can be propagated in the aquarium. Vegetative reproduction of some of these species is commonplace. Aquarium development of larvae that were sexually produced in the wild has been reported many times, often with subsequently successful larval development. I was lucky enough to have wild larvae develop into about three hundred baby orange polyp stony corals, *Tubastrea*, in one of my tanks, and a similar number of unidentified soft corals in another. Several aquarists have successfully reared the extratentacular buds of the stony coral *Goniopora*. I know of one instance in which the West Indian anemone *Condylactis* produced offspring in a hobbyist's aquarium, and I have observed reproduction of the anemone *Phymanthus* in aquaria. Some sea hares (a group of shell-less, herbivorous mollusks) are routinely cultured for laboratory use, as are various echinoderms (the group that includes starfish, brittlestars, sea urchins, sea cucumbers and feather stars). To my knowledge, aquarium culture of large, colorful crustaceans has not been reported, but I am willing to bet that a commercial aquaculturist specializing in food shrimps could succeed with the aquarium shrimps *Stenopus* and *Lysmata*. The future, therefore, looks bright for tank-cultured marine invertebrates. This is fortunate, because we cannot continue to take from the seas as though they were inexhaustible. If we wish to continue to enjoy and learn from the artificial environment of the marine aquarium, we must be responsible stewards of the natural environment, as well. Thankfully, most aquarists appear to share this view.

Chapter Eleven
WHAT YOU SHOULD KNOW ABOUT LIVE ROCK

With the surge in popularity that reef aquariums have enjoyed recently, a lot of folks are talking about "live rock". From the many conversations I have had with aquarists throughout the country, it is apparent that many beginning reef hobbyists, and a few experienced ones, are uncertain about the variety of live rock products that are being offered. Furthermore, there seems to be universal uncertainty about what to expect after live rock is added to the aquarium.

Definition

Live rock is rock removed from the ocean with encrusting plants and animals attached. The nature of live rock can vary due to the following factors:

- **the kind of rock, geologically speaking,**

- **the collecting locality,**

- **the depth from which the rock is taken,**

- **the numbers and kinds of organisms present at the time of collection,**

- **the method of storage and transport of the rock between the collector and the hobbyist,**

- **whether or not the rock is "cured" (see below).**

    With so many variables, it is easy to understand why hobbyists are confused.

    I use the term "live rock" to denote material that is sold in bulk, primarily for the purpose of constructing a "backbone" structure in what is to become a reef tank. This type of rock is generally sold by the pound or in box lots of 30 pounds or so. It may be called "base rock", especially if few organisms are present, or may be described as "decorative rock", or simply "live rock." The name, of course doesn't matter. Rather, of utmost importance to the hobbyist is the treatment that the rock has received between collection and retail sale. You will generally be unable to obtain this information with certainty, and must rely on your experience with your dealer and the information he or she is able to provide concerning your live rock purchase.

Cured Live Rock

The best bulk live rock will have been "cured" for you before you purchase it. Beware, sources may claim that the rock they sell is cured, when, in fact, it is not. The use of uncured rock can be an annoyance, if you were expecting cured material, but is not devastating to a new reef tank. However, the introduction of even a single piece of uncured rock into an established marine aquarium can have disastrous consequences. To understand why this is so, and to better comprehend the nature and purpose of the   curing process, one needs to understand how live rock makes its way from the ocean to your tank.

Few collectors keep their live rock harvest stored underwater between the time it is collected and the time it is shipped to your home town. And no live rock, with the exceptions noted later, is shipped in water. This is to minimize the cost of air freight, a substantial portion of the retail price you pay for live rock. The degree to which the organisms that were originally present on the rock arrive intact in your tank, will depend almost entirely upon how long the rock was out of water between its collection and its arrival in your possession.

Pacific islands are the source for live rock that is formed largely from dead, broken pieces of coral torn from the reef by storms. This "rock" is colonized heavily by pink and purple coralline algae. (This growth, which I regard as analogous to the lichens that encrust trees, stumps and boulders in the woods, is found on most other types of live rock, as well.) In my view, this type of rock is the best choice for creating a reef structure, not only because of its appearance, but also because its irregular shape make building a loose, open "framework" easy to do. Pieces of rock can easily be secured to each other with plastic cable ties, if you are trying to create a dramatic effect.

Rock that is destined to be sold in bulk quantities is generally harvested, roughly cleaned of large organisms, such as seaweeds or big sponge colonies, packed in wet newspaper in insulated boxes, and shipped as soon as possible to the dealer. If the collector must hold the rock for a period of time, it may be placed in tanks or vats -- or it may not. In most cases, by the time it reaches the dealer, the rock will need to be cured before it is placed in your aquarium because it has been out of water for a sufficiently long period to kill some of the organisms present.

Only a few dealers cure rock, because the process is time-consuming and expensive. Curing is absolutely necessary, however, because unless the rock has remained submerged from collection to delivery there will be a significant amount of die-off of the encrusting organisms. This die-off creates pollution, significant quantities of hydrogen sulfide gas (which smells like rotten eggs), and large amounts of organic debris. In the confines of the aquarium, pollution levels will rise above the limits of tolerance of fishes and many invertebrates. Curing must therefore take place in a container separate from the display aquarium.

My procedure for curing live rock is as follows. For 2500 pounds of rock, we use a one thousand gallon system consisting of ten 100-gallon hard rubber vats. The vats are plumbed into a centralized filtration system employing two large bio-towers filled with plastic media, and a large protein skimmer. As soon as rock is received from the supplier, it is briefly rinsed in a bucket of seawater to dislodge sand and other loose material, and placed in the vats. We stack the rock very loosely, to permit maximum water flow around it. At this time, the rock is also inspected for the presence of undesirable organisms, such as crabs or mantis shrimps. Any that are discovered are removed and fed to our triggerfishes. The rock remains in the vat system for two weeks, or longer if necessary. It is inspected periodically and areas of dead organisms, if present, are removed with a brush.

When the curing process is complete, the rock has a fresh, "ocean" smell, and is free of dead, decaying organisms. Few large organisms will be apparent, although the rock still has many spores, holdfasts, and other portions of organisms, from which new macroalgae, and sometimes invertebrates, will grow. In addition, many species of sponges, tubeworms, and miscellaneous other small, encrusting invertebrates survive the curing process and remain on the rock. After the rock is placed in a reef tank, organisms may regrow after several months time.

Another, newer source of bulk live rock is mariculture. When the state of Florida imposed a ban on the collection and landing of live rock in 1992, it also created a provision in its marine resources regulations to permit the production of maricultured live rock. The production of this material involves dumping quarried rock at sea and recovering it several months later, after organisms have had an opportunity to colonize the rock. The basic difference between this kind of live rock and its natural counterpart lies in the kind of quarried rock used. Key Largo limestone, derived from fossil coral reefs, is used for the material I have seen, and the resulting rock is very similar to natural Florida live rock. Only the absence of rounded corners and edges, produced in natural rock by years of wave erosion, enables one to recognize the maricultured product (it has rough, angular, freshly broken edges). The density and kinds of organisms present on maricultured rock will largely reflect the length of time the rock has been under water, as well as the specific geographic locality where the rock was dumped. It is often difficult to pinpoint this information, as locality information especially is kept secret to avoid pilferage. Maricultured rock requires curing, though generally not for so long a time as natural rock. This is because natural rock has many organisms that actually burrow into the rock itself. The most prevalent of these, found largely in rock from the Atlantic and Caribbean, are boring sponges in the family Clionidae. Clionids actually bore holes for their amorphous bodies into solid rock, secreting chemicals which dissolve the rock to make way for the sponge's growth. These sponges will generally die when the rock is left out of water for any but a brief period of time, and are thus a major source of die-off during the curing process. I have observed few boring sponges in rock originating from various localities in the Pacific, interestingly.

Other Rock Products

There are many kinds of decorative specimens for the marine aquarium that come attached to a piece of rock. In fact, it is highly desirable that most of the invertebrates you add to the tank come with a rock "base". Specimens tend to survive better if they are collected with a small piece of the surrounding substrate still attached. It is also vitally important that these specimens be kept submerged in water from the time of collection until their arrival in your aquarium, except for brief periods when transferred from one container to another. If these specimens are handled as though they were fish, they can become striking additions to your reef tank. Almost without exception, these invertebrate communities thrive with minimal care in a properly operated reef aquarium. Light intensity should be high to moderate, water parameters should be very close to the ideals mentioned earlier in this book, and the temperature should be stable, ranging from 74°F to 77°F. Different species of invertebrates will be found on different individual specimens, of course, but here is a list of the most popular types of specimens, with a brief comment about keeping them in the aquarium. As far as I know, all of these live rock community specimens could be kept together in the same aquarium.

Christmas Tree Worm Rock

These come from the Gulf of Mexico, and are characterized by the presence of the Christmas Tree Worm, *Spirobranchus giganteus* . This worm is found in the Pacific, also, usually embedded in *Porites* coral. Such specimens do not seem to be as desirable in the aquarium as their Gulf counterparts, as the *Porites* does not survive well in the aquarium, and its dead skeleton quickly becomes overgrown with filamentous algae. By contrast, the Gulf specimens are usually surrounded by a variety of invertebrates that survive very well, including brightly colored sponge colonies, bryozoans, tunicates, and macroalgae. These are very colorful and desirable specimens.

False or Mushroom Corals

Also from Florida, although further south, comes Florida False Coral, *Ricordea florida* . This is similar to the Mushroom Coral colonies that are obtained from the Pacific. Colonies of flat, disk-shaped polyps cluster on rocks. There is usually a variety of other interesting forms present, although one must wait until the specimen has been in the aquarium for a day or two for them all to settle in, expand, and begin feeding. In the Indo-Pacific region, there are many species of False Corals. All are easily maintained, and will reproduce in the aquarium.

Sea Mats

These, as described earlier, look like colonies of little anemones. They are found in all tropical seas. Specimens of *Zoanthus sociatus* are most commonly collected from the Florida Keys, but Pacific specimens are available in several varieties and have proven easier to keep than this shallow water species. The lemon yellow *Parazoanthus axinellae* is commonly available. Sea mat colonies often share their rocky substrate with other invertebrates.

Soft Corals and Gorgonians

The former are usually attached to a rock, and the latter, especially if not so attached, should be carefully considered only by an experienced aquarist. Gorgonians are more difficult to keep than their fleshier cousins, the soft corals. Most gorgonians come from Florida, while most soft coral specimens come from the Indo-Pacific. A wide variety of other invertebrates may be found tagging along on these specimens, including symbiotic shrimps and crabs. Consult more detailed references for more information concerning specific species of soft corals. In terms of hardiness, they range from the easy to the impossible.

Macroalgae

Rocks collected in shallow water, especially in the Florida Keys, often are covered with a luxuriant growth of many species of macroalgae (seaweeds). While a complete discussion of seaweed culture is beyond the scope of this book, it is worthwhile to point out that such specimens can be extremely interesting additions to the aquarium. Macroalgae require the same high intensity lighting as true corals and some soft corals. Some species of macroalgae will grow so abundantly that frequent pruning is needing to keep them in bounds. A small aquarium devoted to macroalgae and perhaps some of the fish and invertebrate species found in shallow water habitats, can make a beautiful and fascinating display.

These and many other kinds of live rock specimens are available from dealers who stock a wide variety of invertebrates. Remember that most of the organisms mentioned in this chapter *must* be collected still attached to a piece of rock.

In summary, the major difference between live rock that is sold by the pound and live rock that is sold by the piece is that the latter should not have been removed from the water for more than a brief period. Such pieces are handled in the same manner as a fish, and are usually given a descriptive name that refers to the invertebrate type that dominates the fauna on the rock. Rock that has been removed from the water for a period of time must first be cured before it is placed in the aquarium. This rock is sold in bulk, by the pound. Generally, apart from encrustations of coralline algae (which can vary in amount, depending upon the locality from which the rock was collected), no large, showy invertebrates or macroalgae will be present. However, new organisms may regrow on the surface of the rock after it has been in the aquarium for several months. Bulk live rock is used to build a framework upon which other specimens, including other kinds of live rock, may be displayed in a natural setting. For the natural marine aquarium, live rock specimens are not only aesthetically pleasing, but are also fundamental to maintenance of good water quality.

*****

It is my sincere hope that this book will provide everyone who reads it the information necessary to enjoy the exciting hobby of marine aquarium keeping. Only the most fundamental information has been presented, however. I encourage each of you to read as much as you can about marine aquarium keeping and marine organisms, and to develop your own ideas about aquarium management. Good luck in all of your efforts!

Index

A

B

C

About the Author

John Tullock has been a marine aquarist for over 20 years. He holds a Master's Degree in Zoology from the University of Tennessee, where he did scientific research until 1987, when he and several partners founded Aquatic Specialists. Today, Aquatic Specialists is recognized as one of the finest marine aquarium stores in North America, and it serves customers all over the United States through its mailorder division. Tullock's many articles on marine aquarium keeping have appeared in every major hobbyist magazine, and his first book, *The Reef Tank Owner's Manual*, has sold thousands of copies worldwide. He is recognized as an authority on keeping tropical marine invertebrates in home aquariums. When not writing or managing Aquatic Specialists, Tullock enjoys outdoor pursuits, such as hiking, camping in the Great Smoky Mountains, and, especially gardening. He is also a gourmet cook, and is writing a cookbook that is slated for publication in the Fall of 1994. He lives in Knoxville, Tennessee.